CONFEDERATES
DOWNEAST

Commander John Taylor Wood of the *C.S.S. Tallahassee*

CONFEDERATES DOWNEAST

Confederate Operations In And Around Maine

MASON PHILIP SMITH

THE PROVINCIAL PRESS
Portland, Maine

The cover illustration is from a contemporary painting of the *Destruction of the Caleb Cushing* by an unknown artist and is from the collection of the author.

Published by The Provincial Press
519 Congress Street (PO Box 1020)
Portland, Maine, 04104.

Cover Design: Richard Vieira

ISBN 0-931675-09-X

Library of Congress Cataloging-in-Publication Data

Smith, Mason Philip, 1933-
   Confederates downeast.

   Bibliography: p.
   Includes index.
   1. Maine—History—Civil War, 1861-1865—Campaigns. I. Title.
   E511.9.S64   1985   973.7'441   86-30288
   ISBN 0-931675-09-X

Printed In The United States Of America

Dedicated to Dorothea Collins, who so graciously supplied the missing links

"*Altogether it was quite an amusing affair, but I am sorry that I failed, for I did wish to give them some idea of war at their own door, but I trust they will yet experience it; for it will go hard with some of my fellows, if they do not give them a small taste of it, any how, I led the way and the blue cross of the Confederacy did fly over the hills of Maine, in the hands of an armed invader. For I myself did shake it out in the breeze under the flag staff on the hill behind Calais.*"

William Collins, writing from his cell in the Washington County Jail

CONTENTS

INTRODUCTION

The Union vise began to tighten on the South in 1864 as General Ulysses S. Grant's army fought its way through the Battle of the Wilderness and attacked Petersburg, Virginia, where the campaign to capture Richmond bogged down in a nine month siege. Farther South, General William T. Sherman was beginning his march through Georgia, which ultimately led to the March To The Sea. The days of the Confederacy's glory were rapidly waning.

In some areas of the Union there was widespread dissatisfaction with both the purposes and the conduct of the war. This was especially true in parts of Ohio, Indiana and Illinois, all of which bordered on the Great Lakes and were adjacent to Canada.

Confederates in Canada, numbering approximately 15,000 refugees, escaped prisoners, soldiers and secret service operatives, offered the doomed Confederacy a possible means, and a potential base of operations, for a diversionary campaign in the Northern states.

Thousands of Confederate soldiers were being held in prison camps along the Great Lakes. There is some evidence which appears to indicate the Confederate government formulated a plan to free these men, arm them, and utilize them in conjunction with pro-Southern secret societies in the North to foment trouble so that combat troops would have to be diverted from the war front to meet a threat in the rear.

Running the Union blockade of Southern ports, or by stealing through the battle lines, Confederate raiders and agents made their way to Canada, adding to the swelling number of Southerners in the Provinces.

Raids across the Canadian border into Maine and Vermont alarmed the local authorities and made lively reading in the excitable provincial press. This was especially true of the pin-prick Confederate raid on Calais, Maine, a long forgotten incident in Maine's history.

I first read about the Confederate raid on Calais, Maine in 1953 while serving in the United States Air Force in Yongdong-po, Korea. I had just joined a book club and my first selection was a book titled *Confederate Agent* by James D. Horan, the Assistant Managing Editor of the New York *Journal-American*. The National Archives had just opened the long-sealed Turner-Baker Papers to the public and Horan, consulting the papers while researching the exploits of

i

Captain Thomas H. Hines, CSA, for *Confederate Agent*, discovered a long-suppressed file dealing with the Calais raid. Researched only in the National Archives, Horan's two-chapter account of the Calais bank raid raised more questions than it answered.

Who planned and led the raid? Was the border-crossing action approved by Confederate authorities in Richmond? How many Confederates actually took part in the raid? Who were they and what were their backgrounds? Had the authorities in Maine been forewarned of the raid? Was anyone wounded during the raid? Was the raid mentioned in the press at the time, either in Maine or elsewhere in the Union? What was the ultimate fate of the Southerners who boldly raided a peaceful border town in the most northeastern state in the Union at high noon on a hot July day in 1864?

Returning to Maine after studying journalism at Boston University, I remembered Horan's account of the Confederate raid on Calais and decided to investigate the matter further. The Washington County Courthouse in Machias proved a good starting place for my research. Bound volumes of various county newspapers for the Civil War years were stored in a small room behind the second floor court room. The *Calais Advertiser* issues covering the period of the Confederate raid were missing, but other county newspapers reprinted the *Advertiser* account and provided addditional details about the Confederate raid.

I was intrigued to learn, after spending several days immersed in old newspapers, that the Calais affair was only one of several irregular Confederate incidents directed against Maine towns and Maine commerce during 1863 and 1864.

In July of 1863 Lieutenant Charles W. Read, CSN raided Portland harbor and stole the United States revenue cutter *Caleb Cushing* away from her mooring. Five months later Master James C. Brain, CSN, seized the Portland-based steamer *Chesapeake* off Cape Cod while that vessel was on its regular run from New York to Portland. One of Brain's Confederate crew was the brother of Master William Collins, CSN, who led the raid on the Calais bank in July of 1864. A month later, Commander John Taylor Wood, CSN, ravaged Maine coastal shipping with his armed cruiser the *C.S.S. Tallahassee*.

Confederates Downeast is the result my continuing search into the backrounds and actions of these bold Confederates.

Mason Philip Smith, Cape Elizabeth, 1986

ACKNOWLEDGEMENTS

In 1966 DownEast Magazine published a short article of mine about the Confederate raid on Calais. Later, that same year, I presented the annual meeting address of the Maine Historical Society in Portland and spoke about the Calais raid and the devastating cruise of the *CSS Tallahassee* along the Maine coast.

Approximately a year after I presented the annual meeting address, Glenn Skillin, director of the Society, telephoned and asked if I was still interested in William Collins. I replied in the affirmative and he said I should come immediately to the Society's library to meet a Collins descendant.

The descendant was Dorothea Collins, of Chebeague Island, Maine and New Jersey, who had stopped into the Society to inquire about a quilt which had been presented to her grandfather, Reverend John Collins, brother of William Collins the Calais Bank raider, by a Methodist congregation in Harpswell, Maine in 1861.

Dorothea Collins not only knew about William Collins and his service with the Confederacy, but she even possessed several photographs of William in his Confederate uniform and and also owned letters written by William while he was incarcerated in both the Washington County jail at Machias and the Maine State Prison at Thomaston.

In addition, Miss Collins owned an unpublished typecript about the Collins family history, written by Bertrand R. T. Collins, her father, which included a chapter dealing with William Collins. I was fascinated to learn she also possessed several rare Confederate documents dealing with William Collins's appointment as a Master in the Confederate States Navy after he had served in the Confederate States Army.

On a later visit to Portland Miss Collins was kind enough to allow me to photograph many of the documents and photographs in her possession and to graciously give me permission to use them in the book I was planning to write about Confederate operations in Maine. The book has been a long time in production, but I am still extremely grateful to Dorothea Collins for making the the Collins papers available to me.

I would also like to thank W. Neil Franklin, chief of the Diplomatic, Legal and Fiscal Branch of the National Archives; Elmer O. Parker, assistant director of the Old Military Record Division of the National Archives; Allan L. Robbins, formerly warden of the Maine State Prison; Bruce Fergusson, provincial archivist of Nova Scotia; Mrs. Lenore Harrington, librarian, of the Missouri Historical

Society; Leon V. Walker, Jr., formerly assistant attorney general of the State of Maine; John Long of the government documents section of the Portland (Maine) Public Library; Jo Cille Dawkins of the State of Mississippi Department of Archives and History; Charles Haberlein of the United States Navy Audio-Visual Center, Washington, D. C. and Mary Blackford, librarian of the Maritime Museum of the Atlantic in Halifax, Nova Scotia for making items from their various collections available to me.

I owe a special word of thanks to Glenn B. Skillin, former director of the Maine Historical Society, and now associated with the Free Library of Philadelphia, for his assistance and encouragement.

Many individuals, who are not connected with libraries or archives assisted me in the writing of this book by providing inspiration, encouragement and materials over the years. These persons include the late Edward Rowe Snow of Marshfield, Massachusetts; Francis M. O'Brien of Portland, Maine; William C. Darrah, of Gettysburg, Pennsylvania; Lyman Holmes, of Machias, Maine; Dan Poytner of Santa Barbara, California; Marie Melchiori of Vienna, Virginia, and David Hay of Chesham, England.

Peter Dow Bachelder, author of *Lighthouses of Casco Bay* and chronicler of Maine coast shipwrecks; and my father, Guy George Smith, a retired editor and still an active writer at the age of 84, were kind enough to ravage my efforts with their blue pencils. Their constructive criticisms have resulted in a greatly improved book.

My deepest appreciation goes to Barbara, my wife, who has shared with me the joys and frustrations of writing this book. Her good humor and common sense, and her willingness to read and reread my countless drafts of this work, have helped more than I can express here.

Richard Vieira of New Gloucester, Maine designed the cover and selected the text typeface. David G. Engel of Portland, Maine skillfully copied all of the illustrations utilized in the book and made the necessary reproduction photographic prints. Harris G. Smith of Ipswich, Massachusetts, many years ago, exposed me to the professional journalistic standards I have attempted to follow in writing this book. Their contributions are greatly appreciated.

Last, but not least, I am grateful of Adam Osborne for developing the Osborne computer and the concept of bundled software. Without his contribution this book would never have been completed!

CHRONOLOGY

CONFEDERATES DOWNEAST has been written in an episodic manner. Much of the material contained in the six chapters dealing with William Collins and the Confederate raid on Calais, Maine has never been published and includes documents which have never been reproduced. For this reason the book opens with the Confederate raid on Calais and then deals with other Confederate raids and operations in and around Maine.

This chronology will aid the reader in following the actions of the Confederates who raided a Maine town, the harbor of the state's largest city and Maine shipping and commerce. In addition, it will assist the reader in tracing the movements of other Confederate agents in the North, whose movements and actions broadly related to Confederate activities in and around Maine.

1863

May 6, 1863. The *C.S.S. Florida*, off Brazil, captures the brigantine *Clarence*. Lt. Charles W. Read, C.S.N. assumes command of the *Clarence* and sets out to raid along the East coast.

June 12, 1863. Read captures the *Tacony* off Cape Henry and transfers his command to her.

June 26, 1863. Read leads a Confederate raid on the harbor of Portland, Maine. He and his men are captured after seizing and destroying the Revenue Cutter *Caleb Cushing*.

August 16, 1863. Two Confederates escape from their prison at Fort Warren in Boston Harbor. They are later captured in a sail boat off Portsmouth, New Hampshire and are jailed in Portland.

December 8, 1863. John Clibbon Brain, C.S.N., seizes the steamer *Chesapeake* on its run from New York to Portland.

1864

June 18, 1864. William Collins, C.S.N., leads the Confederate raid on Calais, Maine.

August 6, 1864. C.S.S. *Tallahassee*, Captain John Taylor Wood, C.S.N., commanding, runs the blockade from Wilmington, North Carolina.

August 10-12, 1864. C.S.S. *Tallahassee* operates off Long Island, New York and then proceeds to raid shipping along the Maine coast.

August 25, 1864. C.S.S. *Tallahassee* puts into Halifax, Nova Scotia to recoal and replace a damaged spar.

October 11, 1864. The Calais Bank raiders go on trial at the Washington County Court House, Machias, Maine.

October 19, 1864. Confederates, led by Lt. Bennett H. Young, C.S.A., raid St. Albans, Vermont and flee across the Vermont - Quebec border.

November 25, 1864. Confederates, operating from Canada, set fire to New York hotels, Barnum's Museum and barges along the East River.

November 26, 1864. William Collins escapes from the Maine State Prison and makes his way to New Brunswick.

1865

March 25, 1865. Robert Cobb Kennedy, C.S.A., is hanged at Fort Lafayette, New York for attempting to burn New York the previous November.

May 18, 1865. William Collins is paroled by Federal authorities at Grenada, Mississippi.

1866

January - May, 1866. The last of the Calais Bank raiders are pardoned by the Governor of Maine and leave the state.

September 13, 1866. John Clibbon Brain is arrested in the Williamsburg section of Brooklyn, New York and is charged with seizing the *Chesapeake* in 1863 and, without benefit of trial, is placed in the Brooklyn (NY) Penitentiary for three years, making him the last Civil War prisoner.

SEMANTIC NOTE

Several of the events in this book took place in and around Saint John, New Brunswick and that city is frequently mentioned in the text. Various letters, documents and dispatches, in addition to the public press, commonly referred to Saint John by utilizing the abbreviation St., ie., St. John, during the period described in this book. In keeping with the practice of the time, this form has been used in *Confederates Downeast*. Contemporary readers should be aware that Saint John, with the word Saint spelled out, has been the correct usage since early in this century.

CHAPTER ONE

ALARMS ALONG THE BORDER

The *U.S.S. Winooski*, a 240-foot Union gunboat on patrol in the Bay of Fundy, her stars and stripes hanging limply in the hot July sun, eased into St. John, New Brunswick, Canada on a goodwill visit on July 27, 1866. United States Consul James Quay Howard, accompanied by a group of local officials and business leaders, was one of the first visitors to climb aboard when the gangway was lowered.

As the New Brunswickers watched, Captain George H. Cooper presented a massive gold-headed cane to the beaming Consul. Suitably inscribed, this valuable cane was a gift from the grateful stockholders of the Calais (Maine) Bank, whose assets Consul Howard had been instrumental in saving from a band of raiding Confederates two years earlier.

Howard who was retiring after four years as the United States government's representative in St. John, had previously received a letter of appreciation from Joseph A. Lee, the banks's cashier. Lee wrote, "Permit me to express to you the personal obligation I am under to you, as I never doubted that you were the means of saving my life."

James Quay Howard, who preferred to be called J. Q. Howard, had been one of President Lincoln's campaign biographers during the 1860 presidential campaign. Appointed to the critical St. John, New Brunswick post, he was one of the most able Union representatives to serve in the British provinces during the war.   The incredible story behind this letter and the presentation of the gold-headed cane is one of the long forgotten incidents in Maine's Civil War history. Most of the documents dealing with the episode, along with hundreds of other Civil War documents, were sealed after the war to protect innocent people involved in the incident, informers and others loyal to the Union. They were not opened to public examination until 1953.

Consul James Q. Howard, at heart more a secret agent than a diplomat, filled his hours keeping track of Confederates stopping at St. John's hotels and running down rumors of Southern raids to be made against nearby Maine.

Howard, who dined at the Stubbs Hotel, frequently ate with Humphrey T. Gilbert, the St. John Police Magistrate and a personal friend, and thus had inside information about which Confederates were in the city and what they were planning. In addition, Howard had at least one paid informer, and probably more, who provided him with information gained within Confederate circles.

Howard's dispatches to the U. S. State Department in Washington are full of reports of Confederates who passed through St. John. In one case, with the Department's approval, he followed a Confederate Commissioner all the way to Montreal in an attempt to steal important papers from the Southerner.

Stopping in Portland, Maine enroute, Howard obtained the services of John Donahue of Boston, who was able to check into the Commissioner's Montreal hotel to keep track of the Confederate's movements. Howard never was able to steal the papers. All he received for his trouble was a squabble with Donahue over payment for the latter's services.

In May of 1864, Howard, from his St. John office, wrote Assistant Secretary of State Frederick Seward, "Large numbers of disloyal citizens have passed through this city enroute

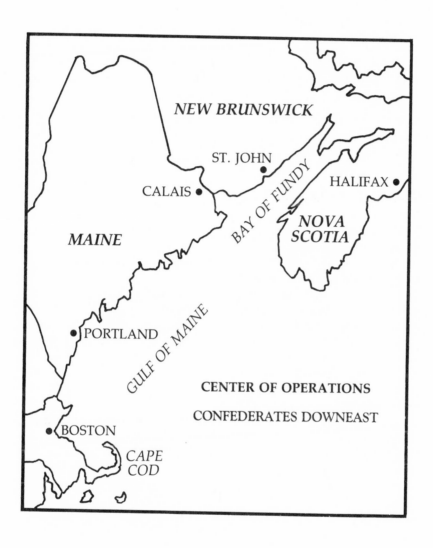

NEW BRUNSWICK

ST. JOHN

CALAIS

HALIFAX

BAY OF FUNDY

MAINE

NOVA SCOTIA

PORTLAND

GULF OF MAINE

CENTER OF OPERATIONS

CONFEDERATES DOWNEAST

BOSTON

CAPE COD

to Canada. In view of these facts, it is possible a raid from Canada upon our Northern frontier may be attempted."

The previous December there had been similar reports of forthcoming raids on the frontier, but they never materialized. However, that same month, sixteen men, mostly New Brunswick citizens under the command of a Confederate officer, seized the New York-Portland steamer *Chesapeake* on the high seas off Cape Cod, Massachusetts.*

Rumors circulating in St. John said this seizure was part of a larger plan to use commandeered vessels to raid towns along the St. Croix River. The steamship *New England*, which ran between St. John and Boston, was also to be taken, according to the rumors.

In response to these rumors, a company of seventy men turned out in Calais and Eastport during a blinding blizzard to defend their homes and property from the expected invaders. In St. John, passengers boarding the *New England* were searched, but only one man was found to be carrying a weapon, a revolver, and the steamer was allowed to sail.

The border quieted down again when the *Chesapeake* was re-taken in a Nova Scotian harbor. But rumors persisted along the Maine frontier that the Passamaquoddy Indians, stirred up by Confederate agents, were planning to rise up and massacre the whites.

Denying the reports, Governor John Francis of the Passamaquoddy tribe said, we "... wish to live in the future as we have in the past, on friendly terms, and to continue that spirit of brotherly love which has forever been cherished and nurtured by our white friends and relatives."

Consul Howard's warnings of raids against the frontier bore fruit when he learned from two different sources that a group of Confederates was completing plans for a raid on Maine.

On July 14, 1864 he wired Governor Samuel Cony in Augusta, the state capital, "A small raiding party left St. John last night to commit depredations on the Maine frontier."

---

*The seizure of the *Chesapeake* is reported in detail later in this volume.

ON DUTY. The citizens of Calais did Guard duty during the nights last week, expecting a raid on the city by "roughs" from New Brunswick.

The editor of the Herald was out all one night "bearing arms" for his adopted country. He says "Hope was entertained that if the invaders were really coming they would come then and there!"

Without any joking the people on the border are really apprehensive of raids from straggling southerners and desperate men who congregate in the cities of the Provinces. Such a state of things is much to be deplored, yet it becomes the curse of all countries devastated by civil wars. If the Administration continues the war for the purpose of subjugation, plunder, robbery and rapine, the state of things of which our neighbors on the border are experiencing, is only the beginning. It is inevitable.

Machias Union reaction to the December, 1863 scare along the Maine-New Brunswick border.

Acting on the basis of this message, the Governor telegraphed the mayors of Maine's principal cities, warning them to put all their forces on alert to resist any attack. In Calais, which could have been attacked by either by land or sea, large numbers of citizens turned out in their shirt sleeves to repel the expected raiders.

The State Guards, under the command of Captain Benjamin Flint, resumed the positions they had occupied the previous December during the *Chesapeake* scare. In their zeal

Author's Collection

Calais, Maine as seen across the St. Croix River from St. Stephen

they even crossed the St. Croix River and took up positions in the neutral town of St. Stephen, New Brunswick.

Further warning of what was coming was given by Consul Howard in a dispatch to the State Department. Rapidly, he wrote, "Satisfactory evidence has been furnished me that one William Collins, late of the rebel army, is now organizing in this vicinity, a force to commit depredations on the Maine frontier. There is reason to believe that the somewhat notorious James McDonald and a precious scoundrel by the name of Jones, are concerned in this new military movement."

Howard closed his report by saying, "Collins is well known here and although a man of energy, is such an eminent fool as to suppose that he can march a small force through the Northern states to Kentucky. He affirms that he is authorized by the 'Confederate authorities' to burn and destroy and to show no quarter."

Howard, in the same dispatch, revealed that Reverend John Collins, William Collins' own brother, had provided the information about the Confederate force being organized in St. John.

The Consul failed to add that David Collins, William's brother, had earlier been one of the men who had seized the *Chesapeake*.

However, before completing the dispatch he wrote:

> Since writing the above I have received information that a small party left St. John last night fully armed and prepared for some desperate enterprise. They represent that they are to be joined in the State of Maine by other men who have come up from the South.

Written on July 14th, this dispatch was not received in Washington until July 19th.

Four days after he sent a warning of a possible raid to Maine's Governor, at 10 o'clock in the morning of July 18th, Howard wired Joseph A. Lee, cashier of the Calais Bank:

> Fourteen men left here in a lead-colored sail and row boat for Calais. Would touch at Robbinston. Intention was to rob your bank in daytime. If they have not been alarmed, you can apprehend them quietly in the bank. William Collins is the leader.

Precisely at noon four men in civilian clothes strode into the Calais Bank, threw some gold coins on the counter and demanded greenbacks in exchange. As they talked with cashier Lee, one of the men moved a hand suspiciously toward his side pocket, which held a small revolver. At the same time, another member of the group cried out a warning to bank officials.

Instantly, the quartet was confronted by weapons in the hands of four men behind the counter. At that same moment a door flew open and other armed citizens rushed into the bank. Gilbert H. Foster of the firm of Foster & Nelson, managed in all the excitement, to wound himself in the foot. He was the only casualty in the raid.[*]

---

[*] On the same morning Mr. Foster shot himself in the foot, other Mainers, members of the 1st Maine Heavy Artillery, in a charge across the battlefield at Petersburg, Virginia, sustained a "record" loss of the war — 635 of 900 men within seven minutes.

CALAIS, July 18.

Three rebel raiders arrested here this morning while attempting to rob Calais Bank.— Names, Collins, Jones, and Philips.

J. S. HAY.

We learn that four men were captured, one of whom was a detective. The plan of the party was to gag the Cashier, close the Bank doors, and rob the institution of the Treasury notes and specie. It failed, however, for as soon as the party entered the Bank they were disarmed and arrested. Collins' name is William ; he is known as Major Collins ; is said to have been in the Confederate service, and is a brother of the David Collins who was concerned in the Chesapeake capture. The affair has caused considerable excitement in Calais.

Probably the residents of Calais themselves will not denounce a plundering expedition of this kind, proceeding from the confines of a friendly country, more vehemently than the people of St. John, among whom the depredators have been sojourning for some time. While there is in the proceeding everything to condemn, we fail to see that it is worthy of being distinguished as a " rebel raid."

The St. John, N. B. *Morning News* account of the Calais Bank raid.

William Collins, the tall, keen-eyed leader of the group, was ordered to hand over his weapons. He coolly replied he had none. But, when the demand was backed up with a revolver, Collins handed over his own revolver and a Bowie knife. A silk Confederate flag was found in his pocket and he boasted he had planned to hang it on the heights of the town.

Defying their captors, the would-be raiders asserted they had planned to rob the bank or post office and burn the town. Still bragging, they claimed they would have succeeded if the additional twenty-five men they had been counting on had reached Calais in time. Each was carrying a revolver and a bowie knife and one had a letter stating they were escaped prisoners of war bent on obtaining funds.

The group also brought along a blank receipt. It was signed with four aliases: Andrew Knapp, Edwin Moore, William Phillips and Jason Videque. This was to be left in exchange for the stolen money.

Intensely excited, a large group of citizens gathered outside the bank. As word of the raider's plot to burn and murder reached the assembled townspeople, some wanted to deal summarily with the raiders right then and there on the main street.

The captors took the raiders to the Municipal Court, pushing their prisoners through crowds of outraged townspeople. At the courthouse the quartet were examined by Judge William Corthell. A St. John policeman, who had arrived in Calais that very morning, told the Judge that Collins had been seen wearing his Confederate uniform. Judge Corthell asked Collins to produce his commission, but the raider was unable to do so. Still boasting, Collins told the judge he and his men had been determined to accomplish their plan"... peaceably if they could but forcibly if they must."

That afternoon, the judge set bail at $20,000, which the raiders could not meet. They were ordered to be held in the Washington County Jail at Machias to await the October session of the Supreme Judicial Court.

THE REBELS IN MAINE.

Attempt to Rob the Calais Bank by Rebels—The Citizens Arming.

CALAIS, Me., July 18, 1864.

At midday to-day there was an attempt to rob the Calais Bank by a small party of rebel raiders, who came here from St. John, N. B. Three men were arrested. The leader of the gang is Collins, a captain in the Fifteenth Mississippi. They say that thirty associates promised to meet them here, but failed.

The vigilance of the State Guard prevented the consummation of this bold scheme of pillage.

The New York *Herald* report of the Calais Bank raid.

CHAPTER TWO

LETTERS FROM JAIL

Rumors were already circulating in Calais that other raiders were on the way to free the prisoners, and the Adjutant General in Augusta detailed fifty additional members of the State Guard to patrol the border.

In Machias, the county seat, a public meeting was held in the grand jury room of the court house to organize a company for the protection of the town against the threatened invasion from across the border. In the nearby town of Eastport 100 rifles were handed out to citizens who signed an obligation to defend the town from Confederate raiders. Further down the coast, at Castine at the head of Penobscot Bay, a Federal gunboat anchored at Dice's Head to protect the port from any marauding Confederate cruisers.

Handcuffed, with their legs securely tied, three of the Confederates were taken under strong guard to Machias in the middle of the night. The fourth man was set free. He crossed the border and returned to St. John, where he checked into Day's Hotel on Union Street.

Several days later, from his new jail cell, Francis X. Jones, the youngest of the trio, wrote his mother in St. Louis to inform her of his plight:

> In Jail, Machais, Me
> July 24, 1864

Dear Mother,

Doubtlessly you will be greatly surprised and grieved to hear from me in such a place. We were captured (myself & companions) on the 18th instant. We are accused of attempting the robbery of the Bank at Calais in this state. We were acting under explicit orders from President Davis. We were also under the command of a regular commissioned officer of the Confederate States Army. Had it been otherwise I would have flatly refused to have joined Captain Wm Collins command when ordered to do so by the confederate authorities. We have been committed to this jail in default of twenty thousand dollars bail, to wait our trial before the Supreme Court in November next. Do not come on here and see me for it would be useless beside being very expensive. So do not come unless I should write and expressly request your presence. Enclose a five to enable me to purchase tobacco, Needles, thread and the other necessities of prison life.

> As ever your affectionate son
> Francis⁻

Two days later Jones wrote another letter from his cell, this time to his former landlady in St. John.

> In Jail, Machias, Maine
> July 26, 1864

Mrs. E. Regan
Madam

All letters that may have arrived for me during my absence, please do up in a bundle and send to my mother Mrs. Lourena C. Jones, in care of Joseph L. Papin, Esq, St. Louis, Missouri, United States of America. You will also send my carpet bag to the same party and address. For your hospitality towards myself during my short sojourn in St. John, I return my sincerest thanks.

Please send all my effects by Express to the above address immediately on receipt of this communication. Please send my shoes and pair of pants hanging behind the door to the following address, Francis X. Jones, care of B. Farrar Esquire, Machias, Washington County, Maine. Send them by express.

Lyman Holmes
This photograph of the cell blocks at the Washington County Jail was taken over 100 years after the Confederate raiders occupied the cells, but the basic structure is as it was in 1864.

Should there be no express running to this place send them home with my carpet bag as directed to the foregoing place.

I would like to detail the circumstances attendant upon our capture, but dare not, for was I to do this letter would never reach you.

My respects to Mr. Brown and sister and to my room mate John Garrick.

You would confer a great honor by sending me St. John newspapers when you can do so.

Please write and inform me when you send my effects to my mother. Please send them immediately on receipt of this.

I am madame
Yours Respectfully
Francis X. Jones

Jones was not the only raider to write letters to the outside world from his cell. William Collins, on the same day, wrote a very interesting letter to his sister in St. John, New Brunswick.

Dear Sister

Here I am a prisoner, how I came here the papers no doubt, have made you acquainted. I failed, "Thanks to all conquering treachery"

What I now wish is that you get some of my friends to write to Richmond, Va. C. S. America to the Hon. S.R. Mallory, Secty. of the Navy. (He is a particular friend of mine) and tell him that I am in this place, with two of my men, Wm. Phillips, and F. X. Jones, the first belonging to a La Regt from N. O. La and the other to the 1st Missouri Regt. both having escaped from Federal prisons; you need not say anything about my Rank, you may if you wish tell him that I formerly was Capt. of Co. (C), 15th Regt., Miss, Infantry, but nothing more, And tell him that the authorities say, that they will not treat us as Prisoners of War, but I have done nothing but what the laws of war, and my instructions warranted, (and am sorry that I done so little) tell him that I lost my papers; but I trust that the President will not allow us to suffer, as Felons and criminals, without informing the Federal authorities, that we were in the lawful discharge of our duties; have two or three letters written least one should miscarry. Send them the usual way

Collins' letter is interesting because of his request that his sister contact Confederate friends in St. John and have them notify the Confederate authorities, in the person of Secretary of the Navy Stephen Mallory, that he had been captured and was not being treated as a prisoner of war. It is also interesting that Collins wanted nothing said about his rank. Formerly a Captain in the 15th Mississippi Regiment and at that time a Master in the Confederate Navy, Collins had been passing himself off in St. John as a Major in the Confederate Army.

He continues by discussing his physical condition:

> I am tolerable well but my cell is cold and damp and I feel a little touch of rheumatism, but that is nothing in wartime.

Mentioning the *St. Croix Herald* account of the Calais raid, Collins uses his letter to set the record straight from his point of view:

> You have in the report that we intended to murder the cashier, but of course no sensible person would believe that we would murder an unarmed and defenseless man. But, if a chance for a successful fight had been given, I have no doubt but my revolver would have brought down five of them for if it had not come in such overwhelming numbers, I would have fought them; but I saw there was no chance to make a successful fight and to prevent a useless flow of blood I surrendered.
>
> As for burning the town, I would have destroyed all the shipping and public property that would not endanger private property; but nothing more, had my men come up, and no traitor been amongst us, we would have been quite successful, but some of my plans were made known to the enemy, and that marred all the next for the present.
>
> Altogether it was quite an amusing affair, but I am sorry that I failed, for I did wish to give them some idea of war at their own door, but I trust they will yet experience it; for it will go hard with some of my fellows, if they do not give them a small taste of it, any how, I led the way and the blue cross of the Confederacy did fly over the hills of Maine, in the hands of an armed invader. For I myself did shake it out in the breeze under the flag staff on the hill behind Calais.
>
> Tell all the folks that Washn is not taken yet, nor Richmond either, for we do not want Washington and they cannot get Richmond.

A portion of the letter William Collins wrote asking his sister to notify Confederate Secretary of the Navy Mallory of his capture. This is actually a copy sent by Washington County Sheriff Benjamin Farrar to the authorities in Washington.

Another letter written by William Collins from his jail cell. This one is in Collins' own handwriting.

Someone in St. John did write to the South on behalf of the captured raider. In another letter written from his Machias cell, on September 22, 1864, Collins told his sister:

> I received your letter a few days ago. I now reply to it. I am glad the matter written of will be attended to. ... You need not be troubled about me for by the help of God and Jeff Davis I will get out of this place by and by. It is not much worse than camp and we have no duty to perform...

Washington County Sheriff Benjamin Farrar, fearful of an attempt to free his charges, placed two guards just outside the prisoners' cells. While armed patrols prowled the streets, a field piece, capable of firing a six pound ball, was positioned in front of the jail. Every townsman who had a gun was requested to be prepared to turn out at a moment's notice to repel any rescue attempt. Members of the Home Guard slept with one eye open, ready for instant action. A month later, rumors were still circulating about a rescue attempt supposedly being planned in St. Andrews, New Brunswick. The plot never materialized.

Some Confederates in St. John might have been planning to free Collins, but others in St. John saw Collins' actions and the entire Calais affair in a different light.

The St. John *Morning Telegraph* commented:

> MAJOR COLLINS AGAIN - There is but one opinion in this community respecting the attempt made by Major Collins of the Confederate Service, and his party, upon the Calais Bank. It is generally regarded as a disreputable effort in the direction of felony, - unbecoming a soldier of the Confederate States, and a man born on British soil. Major Collins arrived in St John about six weeks ago ... What his mission was nobody knew, but some, ourselves among the number, suspected it meant mischief; and gave the Major the benefit of our personal opinion on the subject of "raids" into the United States from British territory, assuring him that public opinion here would not endorse a repetition of the *Chesapeake* case, or any act with hostile intent. We believed that the Major was a gentleman. His appearance indicated as much. He was certainly a military looking man, and appeared to be impressed with proper ideas of honor, as men of his class generally are. We cannot therefore but regret that he has fallen so low as to stoop to the acts of the highwayman, for, as at present advised, his movement resembles nothing else. It is hoped, then, that if, and when, the charges made against the party are established, there will not be the slightest sympathy felt or expressed here for the felons.

CHAPTER THREE

THE RAIDER AND THE MINISTER

Three of the captured raiders were Confederates. The fourth was a Union deserter and informer.

William Collins, the group's leader, was born in 1836 in the north of Ireland. His family had moved to St. John in 1843.and settled in Loch Lomond outside of the city. When Collins was twenty years old he went to New York to further his education and to seek his fortune. While in New York he joined a local militia company, the National Guard of the day, and received military training.

In New York he met John Morrow of Richlands Plantation, Holmes County, Mississippi. Young Collins and John Morrow became good friends and Morrow eventually offered Collins a job as a clerk and bookkeeper in the family business. Collins accepted the offer and moved to Richlands, where he was treated like an older brother and lived in the main house with the Morrow family.

The Morrow plantation was a large one and included a sheep ranch of over 1,000 sheep, hundreds of acres of timber and farmland and a general store which served the surrounding countryside. After five years Collins was taken into the firm of Morrow and Company as a junior partner.

In April of 1861 the Civil War broke out when Confederate forces captured Fort Sumpter. Writing home to his family in New Brunswick that same month, Collins described the Mississippi countryside during that troubled spring:

> ... I only wish you could see something of the country and what they are doing here. ... Now although a great many of the flowers have faded still many more are coming out to replace those that have gone. The Cherokee rose is now in bloom. It bears a large white flower and it is an evergreen shrub and it is used to make hedges and the hedges look like some of your trees in winter, the bottom bright green and the top covered with snow. The air is perfumed with their fragrance. ... The China tree that you read about in "Uncle Tom's Cabin" that grew around Legree's house, grows here and they are beginning to put out their blossoms.

Having painted an idealistic picture of the Mississippi countryside in spring, Collins completed this letter on May 10, 1861 by discussing the war and by revealing he had joined the Confederate Army:

> I will now say something about the war. All the people here thought it would be settled peaceably but I never thought it would. Fort Sumpter has been taken and Fort Pickens is closely besieged by about 10,000 men and there are about 25,000 men assembled at Richmond, Va. About 10,000 men are called from this State and companies and regiments are formed very rapidly. I have been very very busy for two months. I have had to write and keep up my books and also drill men almost every day for I know something about Military affairs. When I was in New York I saw a good many companies drilled and gave some attention to it as well as Fencing, so that I know nearly as much as any of them here and you need not be surprised that I have joined the Confederate Army. I enlisted as a private but my knowledge soon gained me promotion. I first got a Third Lieutenants office but the soldiers were not satisfied with that so they gave me a Second Lieutenants commission and they say they will make me Captain, and where next? So that you see that the-good-for-nothing-fellow at home is good for something abroad, in fact everybody here has a much better opinion of my abilities than I have myself ...

Collins Papers
William Collins in his Confederate Army uniform.

Collins had joined the 15th Mississippi Infantry Regiment, Volunteer, which was organized in May and June of 1861. Quickly elected to a Captaincy, he lost that position when the regiment was re-organized in May of 1862. Twenty-six years old at the time of the raid, his most valuable service to the Southern cause was as a spy after he left the 15th Mississippi.

In another letter sent to his sister in Loch Lomond, written in Jackson, Mississippi, February 7, 1863, Collins told what he had been doing for the past two years and described some of his experiences in the field:

> ... I have been in the 15th Mississippi Regt. and was Captain for twelve months during which time I was engaged nine times against the Federal Forces but was not wounded, but my clothing was cut by shots five times. At the battle of Mill Springs, Ky., our Regt. lost 220 men out of 445, my company lost 27 out of 48. I was the only officer, commissioned or non-commissioned in the company that was not killed or wounded, and there were nine officers with it. I was twice shot at by a soldier from behind a fence about eight paces from me. The first shot killed a man on my right striking him in the head. I then drew my pistol and as he arose from behind the fence to fire again, we both fired together, he fell and his bullet passed so close to my right eye that I could not see out of it for the rest of the day. In making the charge the First Sergt. who was behind me was killed while I escaped, the shot that killed him passing through my clothes. I was in the battle of Shiloh both days, took in 495 men and lost 230. My company lost 26 out of 51 men, I escaped untouched, though we took two batteries and re-took two that were lost. I was in Vicksburg during the siege and was engaged in two attacks on the Mortar Fleet, escaping as usual, for I bear a charmed life.
>
> Give my respects to all my friends, hoping that the war will soon end and that I will go home and stay there, and remain,
>
> Your Affectionate brother,
> William Collins.
>
> P.S. I wrote to you from New Orleans Jan. 18th or 19th but I am now in Charleston, S. C., and send this by a vessel running the blockade, Feb. 18th, 1863.
>
> P.S.#2 I am as mad a secessionist as any Southern Man, and am going to fight out the war and will not return until the Confederacy is acknowledged a nation or conquered and the army dispersed.
>
> P.S.#3 You need not answer this letter by way of the United States.

Captain Collins returned to St. John in the summer of 1863 to visit his family and friends. In the fall he left for the battle

lines again and made his way through the Northern states
rather than run the blockade by sea. Reaching the Confederate lines on September 20th, the day of the bloody Chick-
amauga battle, he passed through Richmond, Virginia the
following day. After the Battle of Missionary Ridge, overlooking Chattanooga, Collins operated in northern Mississippi
and Tennessee as a scout for General Leonidas Polk. Writing
home to friends, he reported he had been offered promotions
several times, but had declined them as he had "something
better in view."

Clues as to Collin's future plans have been found in Civil
War documents still in the hands of his descendants. The
family tradition is that Collins, in conjunction with a Confederate ship, planned a raid on a Maine bank using St. John,
where had friends and contacts, as a base for his irregular
operations.

In order to command a Confederate naval vessel, Collins
would have to join the ranks of the Confederate States Navy.
Through Mississippi friends, Collins, formerly an officer in a
state regiment, sought a naval appointment.

A letter on his behalf, written to a Confederate Congress-
man in Richmond, is still owned by Collins' descendants:

Headquarters French's Division
Brandon, Miss. Dec. 9, 1863

Hon. H. C. Chambers
Richmond, Va.

Dear Chambers:

This will introduce to your acquaintance Capt. William Collins of this state. Capt. Collins commanded a company in the
15th Miss. Vols. during the first year of the war, and served
with the most distinguished gallantry at Mill Spring, Ky., Wild
Cat, Fishing Creek, Vicksburg and Shiloh; and since the spring
of 1862 has been in the Secret Service, penetrating the enemy's
lines and returning with accurate information for Generals
Commanding in the West. He is a young soldier of rare merit, a
man of fine intelligence, of unquestioned nerve and self possession and his resources never fail him in any emergency. I have

known him long and well, and commend him to your kindest consideration.

He visits Richmond for the purpose of securing authority to engage in a naval enterprise which I am satisfied he is eminently qualified to carry out. Give him your influence without hesitation in introducing him to the Authorities.

Your friend,
E. W. Saunders
Major and Adjutant General

On December 18, 1863 William Collins received an appointment as an Acting Master in the Confederate States Navy:

CONFEDERATE STATES OF AMERICA
NAVY DEPARTMENT
Richmond, Va., December 18, 1863

Sir,

You are hereby informed that the PRESIDENT has appointed you

AN ACTING MASTER
In The NAVY of the CONFEDERATE STATES

You are hereby requested to signify your acceptance of this appointment; and should you accept you will sign before a magistrate the oath of office herewith, and forward the same, with your letter of acceptance, to this Department.

S. R. Mallory
Secretary of the Navy

Acting Master William Collins
C. S. Navy

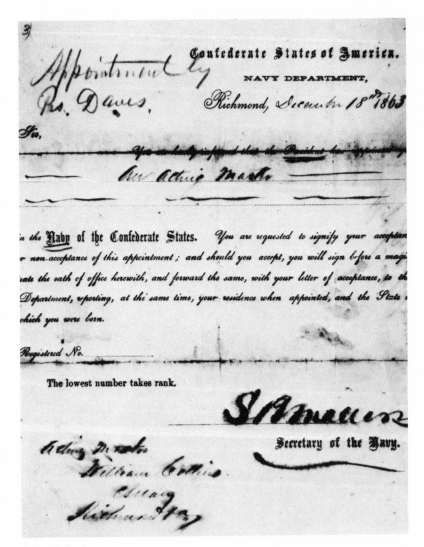

Collins Collection

William Collins' letter of appointment as an Acting Master in the Confederate Navy. The words "Appointment by Pres. Davis" were written on the document in pencil by Reverend John Collins.

Two days after Collins received his appointment in the Confederate Navy he received a hand-written pass through the Confederate lines.

CONFEDERATE STATES OF AMERICA
NAVY DEPARTMENT
Richmond, Va., December 20, 1863

Acting Master William Collins, C. S. Navy, employed on Special Service of importance which renders his passage through our lines necessary, all Military and Naval Commanders of the Confederate States are requested to permit him to pass into the enemy lines.
S. Mallory
Secretary of the Navy

Collins' personal description and statistics are written on the back of the pass:

Description of Person
Height —— 5 feet 11 1/2 inches
Color of eyes —— Hazel
Age —— 26 years
Hair —— Brown
Complexion —— Between Fair & Dark
Signature —— Wm. Collins

In May of 1864 Collins arrived in St. John, having traveled from Alabama, via Vicksburg and Cairo, through the Midwestern and New England states. In St. John, wearing a uniform as a major in the Confederate forces, he boasted he had once spent six weeks as a spy in General George Meade's Union army and that he had also bought his way through the warlines on his way home.

On June 2, 1864, while still in St. John, Collins was appointed as a Master, not in the line of promotion, in the Provisional Confederate Navy. *The Register of the Commissioned And Warrant Officers of the Navy of the Confederate States*, published in Richmond in 1864, under the heading of "Present duty or station" lists William Collins as being on "Special duty".

Collins Collection

William Collins' pass through the lines issued by Confederate Secretary of the Navy Stephen R. Mallory. Again, Reverend John Collins added a comment in pencil.

The records of the Confederate Navy in the National Archives at Washington are very fragmentary and do not include correspondence of the Secretary of the Navy with Collins or documents relating to his appointment. It is only through the zeal of Reverend John Collins that the proof of William's appointment in the Confederate Navy even exists today.

Boasting was probably Major William Collins' greatest fault and it led to his arrest at the Calais Bank. While visiting his sister, Mary Collins, in St. John, he frightened her with tales of his plans to raid Maine. Alarmed, the sister wrote another brother, the Reverend John Collins, 32 years old, who was at the time preaching in York, Maine, "William is home on business for the Confederate army."

The Reverend John Collins was a remarkable man. Born in Ireland in 1832, he converted to Methodism at Collinsville, New Brunswick in 1849. In May of 1852, without money or friends to help, he entered the Maine Wesleyan Seminary at Kents Hill, Maine, where the principal, Dr. Torsey, took him under his wing. Three years later, John Collins was licensed to preach and began to ride the Maine circuit.

July of 1864 found Reverend Collins serving a church in York, Maine, a coastal community near the New Hampshire border. Reading the letter from his sister, Mary , the minister learned his younger brother William, whom he thought was fighting in the South, was home and attempting to "kindle a back-fire of some kind."

The minister told his wife he would have to hurry to St. John to see what William was planning. Short of funds, having only $5.00 in his pockets, he appealed to his congregation, meeting the next day for regular Sunday worship, for money for the journey. Moved by his request, the parishioners contributed $35.00 towards his travel expenses.

Immediately upon arriving in St. John, Reverend Collins hurried to his sister's home. William was not there and his sister said he was "out drilling some desperate characters." Mary showed the minister William's room, where they found a map of Maine spread out on a table. Mary said that she had overheard William telling some of his men "the vessel had not come," but she also said that she did not know what vessel was being discussed.

Chestnut Street Church
The Reverend John Collins as he appeared many years after the Calais incident.

John was convinced trouble lay ahead and decided he "must play an important part" in preventing that trouble.

William returned to the house later that evening and the two brothers, who had not met in several years, chatted pleasantly. The minister tried to sound out the keen-eyed William, but the Confederate plotter was careful not to say anything to commit himself. John Collins said the North was certain to win the war, which brought a quick response from William that the older brother was mistaken.

His eyes flashing, William proclaimed the soldiers in gray were better fighters than those in blue. In a bold affirmation of his statement, William pulled a silk Confederate flag from his pocket and waved it in the minister's face. John leaped to snatch it away from his brother, but the latter stuffed it back in his pocket and the pair continued to argue until long after midnight.*

During the course of their discussion, John Collins said to his brother, "I don't know what your plans are, but I shall do all in my power to block them. Knowing that you are a spy, I should be a traitor to my country if I did not deliver you over to the hands of the authorities!"

The brothers failed to attain a meeting of minds. Reverend Collins, turning to what he knew best, reminded William that in their old home they had always said their prayers before retiring. Both dropped to their knees and voiced an impassioned prayer. However, the joint effort failed to calm Reverend Collins. He laid awake all night trying to determine what project William was planning to aid the Southern rebellion.

The next morning the minister hurried to Consul Howard's office on Prince William Street and told him what he suspected about William's plans. Howard told the minister he would look into the matter.

---

*Several designs of Confederate flags were in use at the time. The "Stars and Bars," had two horizontal stripes of red separated by a white stripe of equal width, and a circle of white stars in a dark field in the upper left corner. The "Battle Flag" was a red square, crossed diagonally with two blue bars, with thirteen white stars on the blue. A rectangular version of this flag served the Navy as a jack. William was carrying the "Battle Flag".

The following day at Howard's request, Reverend Collins returned to the Consul's office. Much to his surprise he found two other men in the office. Both were dressed in civilian clothes, but they were American steamship captains. One was Captain Field of the *New England* and the other was Captain Winchester of the New York boat.

The four discussed in detail Reverend Collins' information about his brother. Writing about the meeting years later, the Reverend said:

> We discussed the matter thoroughly with the result that we put several able detectives on the track of Captain William with orders to dog his every movement and find out his plans. These detectives came into the good graces of my brother and became his pals and members of his company. They also found out that his plan was to capture the Calais Bank, where a large amount of gold was stored. A vessel was to be in readiness to take this gold at once to some southern port. It was a well laid scheme and would have been successful had not the plot been discovered.

CHAPTER FOUR

TWO CONFEDERATES AND AN INFORMER

Francis X. Jones, the young Confederate captured in the ill-fated raid on the Calais Bank, had the most exciting career of the trio. The son of the Marshal of the Missouri Supreme Court, and a jeweler by trade, 21 year old Jones had run away from home as a teenager to marry Gabella J. Carson, his childhood sweetheart, and to fight in the Missouri-Kansas border wars. Later, his wife and child were killed by troops under the command of Jim Lane, a Kansas guerilla leader.

Following two years of study at St. Louis University, where he mastered French and German, young Jones joined the Dixie Guard, Company G, 2nd Regiment of the Missouri Volunteers. This organization, which was part of the State Guard, was captured at Camp Jackson, St. Louis in June of 1861 when Federal forces under Captain Nathaniel Lyon moved against pro-secessionist state troops who were planning to seize the St. Louis Armory. The state forces were released after taking the oath of allegiance to the Federal government

With the formality of pledging allegiance to the Union behind him, Francis X. Jones, still a strong Southern supporter, traveled south to Memphis, where he joined the First Missouri Regiment, Confederate Service.

Moving ever southward, the First Missouri operated in Kentucky, Tennessee, Alabama and Mississippi until it was engaged at Shiloh, where Jones was wounded in action. Crippled, he regained his strength in hospitals in Oxford and Canton, Mississippi. Discharged from field service, Jones was sworn into the Confederate Secret Service on July 3, 1863.

Completing a sixty day furlough in Canton, Mississippi, he proceeded north on his first secret service mission. This was to carry letters and dispatches to Southern agents along the Mississippi River and to a Major Morris in Chicago. Before his capture at Calais, Jones made thirty-two trips through the Union lines with dispatches and twice made trips to Canada.

Concluding the first of his Canadian assignments, Jones returned to the South by running the Federal blockade of Southern ports. After delivering dispatches in Montreal he boarded the steamer *Caledonia* at Quebec to go to Halifax. Arriving at that Nova Scotian port, he was met by Alexander Keith, the regional Confederate agent, who put him on a ship bound for St. George, Bermuda. Major Norman S. Walker, the resident Confederate agent at St. George,* then put Jones aboard the steamer *Emily*, which ran the blockade to Wilmington, North Carolina.

In his travels behind Union lines, Jones used such aliases as Jason Videque, Allanna F. Jones, Charles K. Faulkner, Francois F. Marceau and Dr. J. K. Frank.

On his second trip to Chicago, Jones again delivered packages to Major Morris in a saloon. He then traveled to Montreal, where he reported to a Mr. C. Slaughter, another Confederate agent. Slaughter passed Jones, along with a Lieutenant Ream and a Major Harris, on to Benjamin Weir, the Confederate agent in residence in Halifax.

Evidently the Canadian authorities kept a sharp eye on Jones and his movements in their territory. In a report about

---

*Walker's headquarters were located in the Globe Hotel. Today the building houses an interesting Confederate Museum with an engaging collection of exhibits from the Civil War period.

Jones and his travels written by the St. John police chief to the Provincial Secretary after the Calais bank raid, the police chief reported:

> The man Francis X. Jones is a native of St. Louis, Missouri; and left there early in April last, and arrived in Montreal on the 21th of same month - remaining there until 29th. Then he started for Quebec. He left Quebec on 30th April for Halifax, from which latter place he arrived in St. John on 23rd June, where he remained until he left for Calais on 14 instant.

While waiting for a ship in Halifax, Jones decided he had had enough of the secret service life. On May 28, 1864, he wrote to President Abraham Lincoln asking for a pardon under the terms of the President's Amnesty Proclamation. In his letter he said:

> All I ask is to be allowed to remain in peace on my mother's farm and conduct the business thereof unmolested ... and also to be exempt from all military service.

He told the President he had been transferred to the secret service without his consent and had nothing "to plead in extenuation of my fault save my youth and inexperience and the cajolery of those who know how to entrap the un-suspecting."

The War Department replied on June 11th, but declined to grant amnesty on the grounds Jones had asked exemption from military service. He was informed "...it is not deemed expedient to confer the privileges of citizenship upon anyone who at the same time solicits exemption from its duties and responsibilities."

Somehow, Weir and Keith, the rebel agents in Halifax, discovered Jones had written President Lincoln; and the young dispatch carrier was ordered to join William Collins in St. John.

Jones already knew Collins, having seen him once before on Mississippi's Yazoo River. Collins was then with a squad of "banditti" men, probably guerillas. Collins explained to Jones, after the latter arrived in St. John, that he, Jones, was to take part in a series of squad-sized raids to destroy "public property and corporation property."

Little is known about William Phillips, the second member of the raiding party, other than he was an obstinate, ignorant and reckless man from New Orleans.* He had been a sailor before joining Collins in St. John. An Irishman like Collins, he had been a member of the Ninth Louisiana Regiment before turning to the sea.

The fourth man with the party at the Calais Bank was William Daymond, a deserter from Co. H, 6th New Jersey Volunteers. He had been working as a potter in St. John after he skedaddled * on August 16, 1862 on the march from Harrison's Landing, Virginia during the bloody Peninsula Campaign.

Daymond's personal background is almost as interesting as that of William Collins and Francis X. Jones. He was a native of Plymouth, England, who emigrated to the United States in May of 1859. Six months later he entered the U. S. Navy and served until he was discharged in July of 1861.

He then enlisted in the U. S. Army, 6th New Jersey Volunteers and remained with his regiment for eleven months before deserting. Wandering behind the Confederate lines, Daymond was captured at Winchester, Virginia on August 27, 1862 and placed in Libby Prison in Richmond.

Daymond, according to a Confederate document on file in the National Archives in Washington, told the Confederates he had deserted the Union cause because "they were fighting for negroes." He was held in prison for five months for "coming over." However, the Confederates must have believed his story for he was released and given a passport to go to Augusta, Georgia. In Augusta he reported to the mayor, who suggested Daymond go to Savannah and enlist to serve on the privateer *Nashville*.

---

*This description of Phillips was written by Assistant Judge Advocate Levi C. Turner-,USA in a report written by Turner after he interview the Calais bank raiders in their Machias cells. Turner's Machias interiews are discussed in detail in the following chapter.

*Ie., deserted and fled to Canada. The term usually refers to draft-dodgers. According to historian Robin Winks, so many draft-dodgers settled around Mapleton, New Brunswick that the area was called Skedaddle Ridge. There was also a Skedaddler's Reach on Campobello Island, N. B., which lies opposite Lubec, Maine.

The *Nashville* was a brig-rigged passenger steamer which before the war ran between New York and Charleston, S. C. After the fall of Fort Sumpter she was seized by the Confederates and turned into a cruiser. Renamed the *Rattlesnake* she was re-commissioned a privateer in November of 1862. Daymond served on the *Rattlesnake* until she was destroyed by Union forces in the Ogeechee River, Georgia on February 28, 1863.

Daymond returned to Charleston, where he worked for two months on the *Kate*, which had been wrecked in the Cape Fear River. He then made his way to Richmond, where he was arrested by the Confederate authorities as a "suspicious character. " However, his various papers and passports checked out and he was released. Having served in two opposing navies and in the Union army, where he was still listed on the rolls as a deserter, Daymond decided to leave the war and made his way to neutral New Brunswick.

It is not known how Daymond came to the attention of Consul Howard, but after Reverend Collins told Howard about the projected Maine raid the Consul sought out Daymond and asked him to join the gang as an informer. Daymond did his job well and kept Howard informed of the gang's plans. It was this precise information that enabled the Consul to alert the authorities about Collins' exact objective.

Not everyone in St. John praised Daymond for his efforts on behalf of Consul Howard. The St. John *Morning Telegraph* of July 24, 1864 published the following letter to the editor:

Beware of Detectives!

To The Editor of the Telegraph.

The party who acted with Collins, Jones and Phillips in their contemplated robbery, and betrayed them to the American Consul, is a man named Dayman (sic). He is a potter by trade, and was for some time in the employment of William Warwick. He makes no attempt to conceal the part he played in that affair, and acknowledges he entered into the plot and accompanied the parties to Calais. At present he is boarding at Day's Hotel on Union Street. Persons who do not desire to be led into plots, conspiracies, and so forth, should, after posting themselves upon his personal appearance, give him a wide berth ever after.

In this neutral City, we do not desire to take part in any schemes planned against our neighbors. Neither should thoughtless persons among us so conduct themselves ultimately to walk into the traps prepared for them by the Consul.

Considering the large number of suspicious characters from the States now here, would it not be well for a number of our citizens to form themselves into a Vigilance or Home Protection Committee, to prevent the recurrence of such outrages as have lately taken place.

Paul

Perhaps there was a quid pro quo involved between Howard and Daymond for on August 25 the former sent a dispatch on Daymond's behalf to the State Department:

I have the honor to request that William Daymond, late a private in the 6th Reg. New Jersey Vols., be furnished with a pardon for the offense of desertion and exempted from the penalities, to which he would otherwise be liable, for said offense.

The grounds upon which this request is presumed are these:

1. During the time of the recent disturbance at Calais, Maine, Daymond with his own free will furnished me valuable information and kept the authorities at Calais and the officials of the Calais Bank thoroughly informed concerning the movements of the Confederate thieves and as a result of the precautions taken by him I have no doubt the life of the cashier of the Calais Bank was preserved and possibly the town itself.

2. Daymond expresses and I believe, entertains, a strong desire to return to his regiment and take part in the contest, as soon as his services are no longer needed as a witness in the prosecution of William Collins et al.

Howard's dispatch regarding Daymond was received in Washington on August 31. The original dispatch is in the National Archives in Washington and a hand-written note at the top of the original states " Copy to the War Dept."

William Daymond, formerly of the 6th New Jersey Volunteers, deserter and informer, was granted a full pardon by the War Department on September 13, 1864.

CHAPTER FIVE

THE INCREDIBLE PLOT

Young Francis X. Jones, sitting in his cold and dark cell in Machias, decided he would try once again to leave the Confederate secret service and either return to Missouri or join the Union forces. Previously, he had written directly to President Abraham Lincoln, requesting he be allowed to join the army.

This time he began his campaign on the local level by writing an intriguing letter to Sheriff Benjamin Farrar, his jailer:

> Mr. Farrar:
>
> Having for sometime been importuned by my mother to leave the Rebel Army, and my own inclinations leaning the same way, I have determined so to do, and being desirous of entering the Union Army, I ask your assistance in so doing, therefore I most earnestly request you to represent my desire to the proper authorities.
>
> I am furthermore in possession of facts which if made known to the proper authorities in time will enable them to defeat the plan of operations of a very powerful conspiracy extending throughout the free states and British Provinces. I can put them

in possession of the names of some of the principal men or movers of the said conspiracy in New York, Boston, Portland, Halifax, Pictou, St. John, Quebec, Montreal, Windsor and various other cities throughout the North.

I will reveal all that is known to me immediately on entering the army. Once I make known the facts in my possession, and it would come to the knowledge of the Rebel Agents or their co-insurrectionists in the North that I was the person that revealed them, my life will be sought & constantly beset by their secret emissaries who are many and powerful.

Therefore I would request that my name be kept from them if possible.

I have, poor fool that am, been made a tool of by scheming ambitious men, and now that I have awakened to the sense of my situation, I mean to pay them in their own coin.

Respectfully requesting your earliest attention in my behalf,

I am Sir your etc
Francis X. Jones

Several days later Jones, not having received a reply from the sheriff, wrote another letter. In it he offers to make a partial disclosure of his information and claims to fear his fellow Calais raiders:

Being fearful that the answer to my proposal will not arrive in time to prevent certain movements enemical (sic) [inimical] to the interest of the Government I have resolved to make a partial disclosure of the aforesaid movements. Therefore I request you to bring in the Provost Marshal that I may do so. I also request you to remove me from my present place of confinement to some place more distant from Collins and Philips, for I would not have them know my movements for I know them to be most desperate men, therefore I will acknowledge to you that I fear them more than the Devil himself.

Jones closed with another offer to disclose all he knew about the forthcoming Confederate efforts:

I beg you to inform me of the decision of the Authorities in regard to my communication at as early date as possible. If they see proper to grant my request I will reveal all I know which will be more than sufficient to enable them to defeat the said movements. Of my ability to do so I will furnish them the best of evidence and will answer for its truth with my life.

Trying another tack, Jones wrote a third letter, this time to Washington County prosecuting attorney Charles Whidden. He began by making a long statement explaining the methods used by Confederate agents carrying dispatches through the battle lines and then attempted to boost his importance by claiming a series of promotions while in the Confederate service:

> My rank in the regular field service of the rebels was first corporal. This position I resigned. I was afterwards appointed sergeant and on entering the secret service I obtained the rank and pay of captain ...

Alarmed by Jones' letters, Sheriff Farrar wrote Secretary of State William H. Seward, outlining the Confederate plot as told to him by Jones. Farrar also urged the Secretary of State to send a detective "or other authorized employee of the Government" to Machias to investigate Jones' claims.

Seward replied "The information ... is deemed important and ... your suggestion as to the method by which additional facts may be obtained, will be duly considered.

Sheriff Farrar also wrote to Secretary of War Edwin M. Stanton. Stanton replied, requesting Jones be transported to Washington for interrogation by the Federal authorities.

Assistant Secretary of War Charles A. Dana also sent a letter to the Washington County sheriff:

> War Department
> Washington City
> August 22, 1864

> Sir,
> Your letter of the 16th inst., addressed to the Sec of State, has been referred to this Dept. The Sec of War desires that if possible the prisoner Jones, now in your charge, should be brought here for examination concerning the matters spoken of in your letters. If you can bring him here, all expenses, with suitable

compensation to yourself, will be paid by this Dept. On arriving here, Jones may be committed for safe keeping to the Old Capitol Prison and after his examination can be taken back to the jail in Washington County if necessary.

Yours very respectfully,

C. A. Dana
Asst Sec of War

The sheriff replied on August 29th and refused both Stanton's and Dana's requests to send Jones to Washington. Fearful Jones might escape while in Federal custody, the small-town minded Farrar wrote:

> The party referred to is the most desperate one of the three confined here on the charge of an attempt to commit the robbery of the Bank. If, by any possibility, he should escape from the persons having him in charge, I fear I should be held personally responsible.*

Receiving the sheriff's final words on the matter, Assistant Secretary of War Dana capitulated and ordered Assistant Judge Advocate Levi C. Turner to Machias to interrogate Jones and the other raiders.

Both Collins and Phillips refused to make any statement to the Federal investigator from Washington. Jones gave a twenty page statement detailing the Confederate plot against Maine and gave minute details of his own career in the Confederate service.

Jones told Turner that just before the November presidential election there was to be a series of uprisings by members of disloyal groups in Maine, Michigan, Ohio, Indiana, Illinois, Iowa and Missouri. They were to destroy and burn government warehouses, banks, railroads and other public property, with the ultimate aim being nothing less than the overthrow of the Union government.

---

*In a letter to the author, dated March 28, 1984, Machias attorney and local historian Lyman Holmes wrote: "Regarding Farrar's concern about transporting Jones to Washington, it is interesting to note that Farrar was being sued at this time due to the failure of one of his deputies to properly attach a lien on anchors, cables and chains of a vessel. ... Perhaps due to this case, Farrar was not about to stick his neck out and get in more problems."

War Department
Washington City.
September 5th 1864

Major :

You will proceed with all reasonable dispatch to Machias, Washington County, Me, to investigate there the cases of Collins, Phillips and Jones, and make report to this Department.

By order of the Secretary of War

C. A. Dana.
Asst. Secretary of War

Major L. C. Turner,
Associate Judge Advocate

War Department orders to Major Levi C. Turner to travel to Machias, Maine to investigate the Calais raiders' cases.

The attack against Maine, as related by Jones and as incredible as it now seems, was to be made by 5,000 men, supported by field artillery. This force was to be commanded by experienced officers from the staffs of Generals Wheeler, Morgan and Stuart. The raiding party and the artillery were to be carried to Maine by eight armed blockade-running steamers.

Landing at five points along the coast, within supporting distances of each other, the troops' orders were to scour the countryside for horses and to link up with members of the secret societies before beginning a campaign of guerilla warfare.

Jones claimed fifty experienced engineers and topographers had left for Maine on May 18th to map unfrequented sections of the coast. Turner's pen flew across the paper, writing down the whole implausible story. The prisoner said he had seen several charts made by these engineers while he had been a private secretary to a high Confederate officer.

In connection with this expedition there was to be another comprised of 1,200 to 1,500 men. This group was to embark for Maine in sailing vessels, escorted by two Confederate cruisers, the *C.S.S. Tallahassee* and the *C.S.S. Florida.* Originally this force was to consist of 2,000 men, but it was decided to divert 500 of them to mount an offensive against the prison camp at Johnson's Island, Ohio to take attention away from the attack on Maine.

Despite the apparently well laid plans, the armed invasion of Maine never materialized beyond the planning stage. But, it is interesting to note an attempt was made that September to free the prisoners at Johnson's Island. Also, an attempt was made to free the prisoners at Camp Douglas near Chicago.

Expanding on his statement to the Assistant Judge Advocate, Jones provided names and complete descriptions of the rebel agents who were operating in the Canadian provinces and in the Northern states. Some of the men, like Benjamin Weir in Halifax, he knew from his missions as a dispatch carrier; others, like Colonel J. D. Martin in Boston, he had known during the Mississippi campaign. Once, in Jackson, Mississippi, he had given Martin directions for the best routes through the Union lines.

to them from southern generals; and who, as he
declares, are stationed at various points at the
North, for the purpose of facilitating correspondence
and communication with the South — aiding the
transportation of contraband goods and the running of the blockade — collecting deserters from
the rebel army, &c, &c. He presents their names
and stations as follows.

    Portland, Me. — Major Dudley Harris — alias
    'Spencer,' alias 'Barbour'
    Boston — Col. J.O'C Martin.
    New York — Col. Geo. & Maj. A. Hawthorne.
    Brooklyn, N.Y. — J. Taylor, tavern-keeper.
    Philadelphia — Maj. Chas. Rice.
    Baltimore — Col. Wm. Hamilton.
    Chicago — Maj. Morris or Maurice, — alias
    'Sam Ober'
    Springfield, Ills. — Capt. Thos. Shiver, alias
    'Oliver Ditson'.
    St. Louis — Wm. Kendall and Capt. Lewis
    Kennedy.
    St. Joseph, Mo. — John or Wm. Ritchie.
    New Madrid — James Hunter.
    Cape Girardeau — Col. Wm. Harper.
    Memphis — Capt. Pope.
    Nashville — Col. Thos. J. Tunstall.
    Cincinnati — Maj. Haskemore.

National Archives

**A detail of Major Levi C. Turner's report to the War Department in
which he lists the names of Confederate agents supplied him by
Francis X. Jones.**

One of Jones's best descriptions of a Confederate agent operating in the North is that of Major Dudley Harris, who used the aliases Spencer and Barbour. Harris, a relative of Colonel Martin in Boston, operated in Portland, Maine. He was about 35 to 40 years old. Jones said he had "... a bulldog look; snuffs up his nose; squints with his left eye when looking intently at anyone; dark hair slightly tinged with grey, dark eyes, and I think has a slight scar under the right eye.'

It was through the efforts of such men as Dudley Harris and Colonel Martin that members of the various Copperhead secret societies, like the Knights of the Golden Circle and Sons of Liberty, communicated with the Confederate government in Richmond.

According to Jones, rebel agents carrying British passports had left St. John during the past three or four months to contact members of the secret organizations in the states bordering the British provinces to secure men as guides and spies for the Southern troops who were supposed to land in Maine.

Swearing his twenty page statement was "full and true", Jones protested he had been "seduced from his allegiance to the Union by wicked and designing men who capitalized on his youth and inexperience." Hopeful that his United States citizenship would be restored, he said he was now willing to enter the armed forces, preferably the Navy, as atonement.

Enroute to the mill town of Lewiston in SouthCentral Maine, where he was to investigate irregularities in the draft, Assistant Judge Advocate Turner wrote a report of his interview with Jones to Secretary of War Edwin M. Stanton. He reported he had been able to verify some of Jones's statements by consulting with the provost marshal in Portland.

During the past two months, according to the provost marshal, a person had often picked up mail at the Portland post office addressed to Dudley Harris. The young Jones' statement was further corroborated when Turner learned that several persons posing as artists had been discovered surveying and mapping the deserted bays and harbors along the Maine coast.

Turner recommended the Federal authorities should seriously consider Jones' statements and also observed:

> This statement of Jones, corresponds, in many particulars, with official information in my possession; and taken in connection with facts that may be in the possession of the War and State Departments, it may be important and if so, require prompt action.

Concerning the Confederate cruiser *Tallahassee*, Turner wrote "... he (Jones) states that the *Tallahassee* is one of the steamers to be used to convoy the raiding party on vessels — and the *Tallahassee* has been along this coast — but Jones was placed in jail last July, and did not know that piratical steamer has been here, and does not, now, know it."

CHAPTER SIX

THE TALLAHASSEE AND FLORIDA

While the *Tallahassee*, a twin- screw, 700-ton, two hundred foot armed cruiser, never did convey a raiding party to the Maine coast, she did wreak havoc among coastal shipping. She accounted for the destruction of three ships, three barks, one brig and twenty schooners. Paroled on their oath not to take part in the war, the captured vessels's crews were sent in small boats to the tiny fishing community of Friendship, Maine.

Built in England for the opium trade, the *Tallahassee*, originally known as the *Atlanta*, had previously been utilized as a commerce-carrying blockade runner. From April to July 1864, during the height of her blockade running days, the *Atlanta* made four fast trips between Bermuda and Wilmington, North Carolina carrying preserved meat for General Lee's Confederate army.

Her final clandestine voyage ended on July 14th, four days before the Calais bank raid, when she docked in Wilmington, North Carolina. There, she was pressed into regular Confederate service by the government, who paid $125,000 to the blockade running firm of Peters, Stevenson and Wilson Company. Her former owners realized a profit of $40,000 on the sale.

Using the former blockade runner as an armed cruiser the Confederates planned to carry the war direct to the Union's coast. She was re-commissioned the *Tallahassee*, on July 20, 1864, two days after the raid on the Calais Bank.

The *Tallahassee* was a first-class, extremely fast, well constructed vessel. She made fourteen and a quarter knots on her trial run. Her two engines could be either worked together or separately. This twin-screw system replaced the former unprotected paddle wheel system of propulsion. However, her boilers were not protected from enemy fire and were designed for trips of less than 1,000 miles, which greatly reduced the low silhouetted cruiser's range.

To protect the vulnerable boilers, cotton bales and an extra supply of bagged coal was stacked on the deck. The valuable coal would provide added protection to the ship and its crew until it had to be utilized to extend the vessel's fighting range.

The new Confederate cruiser's armament consisted of one rifled 100-pounder amidships, one rifled 32-pounder forward and one long Parrott gun aft.

The hand-picked crew of 120 officers and men was paid in gold and most came from the James River Squadron. They included a small group of marines, who were placed on board to act as sharpshooters and who would swing into action when boarding parties were needed to seize enemy ships.

Colonel John Taylor Wood was selected to be the *Tallahassee's* first commander. Wood already had enjoyed a distinguished career when he took command of the converted Confederate cruiser. His father was Surgeon General Robert C. Wood of the United States Army. His mother was the daughter of President Zachary Taylor and the sister of the first wife of Jefferson Davis, the Confederate president.

John Taylor Wood, a midshipman in the United States Navy during the Mexican War, was Assistant Professor of Gunnery and Seamanship at the United States Naval Academy when the Civil War broke out. Resigning his commission, he enlisted in the service of Virginia and was a lieutenant on the *Merrimac* during its famous battle with the *Monitor*.

He was later assigned to the staff of President Davis and given the rank of Colonel of Cavalry. Before taking command

Stephen R. Mallory   **Gideon Welles**
Confederate Navy Secretary   **Union Navy Secretary**

of the *Tallahassee* he led numerous water-borne expeditions against the Union forces on Chesapeake Bay.

Wood's orders from the Secretary of the Navy Mallory were general in scope and included this observation:

> The character and force of your vessel point to the enemy's commerce as the most appropriate field of action, and the existing blockade of our ports constrains the destruction of our prizes. ... Relying confidently upon your judgement and ability and believing that the untrammelled exercise of your own wise discretion will contribute to your success, it is deemed unnecessary to give instructions for your cruise.

Wood was the ideal commander for the South's visionary threat to Union shipping. Years later, writing about his exploits in *Century Magazine*, Wood said:

> The Captain of a successful blockade-runner needed to be a thorough seaman and a skillful navigator. His work required a boldness, decision in emergencies, and the faculty of commanding men and inspiring the confidence of his crew. ... That absence of these qualities would invite loss was made apparent

in a great number of instances, when the steamers were almost thrown away by bad landfalls, or by the captain or crew wilting at the first sight of a cruiser or the sound of a gun.

On a high tide and under a moonless sky, John Taylor Wood and the *Tallahassee* set out to sea on August 4, 1864 and promptly grounded on a sand bar. She was pulled free two hours later, but a receding tide forced a 24 hour delay and even then the proud cruiser grounded so fiercely that three steamers strained mightily before pulling her free. Finally, On August 6th, the *Tallahassee* skimmed over the treacherous coastal sands and made for open sea, where she eluded the Union blockade fleet of more than fifty vessels positioned throughout an area extending up to 100 miles from shore.

The next few days passed uneventfully, with Wood sighting and speaking to several foreign ships. From one, the Confederate captain obtained the latest New York newspapers.

Steaming northeastward on August 11th, within eighty miles of New York, the *Tallahassee* took its first prize, the schooner *Sarah A. Boice* of Boston, bound for Philadelphia in ballast. The *Boice's* crew, together with their belongings, were brought on board the cruiser and the schooner was scuttled. The prisoners were allowed to keep their money, watches and clothes, but the Confederates seized the vessel's chronometer, charts and medicine chest.

Steaming toward Fire Island Light, on the Long Island shore, Wood sighted seven vessels, one of which altered sail and headed for the *Tallahassee*. Wood recognized her as a pilot boat, which soon luffed under his ship's quarter, allowing the black-suited pilot to step aboard the larger vessel.

As he stepped aboard the pilot glanced at the ship's flag, which was unfolding in the slight breeze.

Turning to the smiling Wood, he exclaimed "My ____! What is that? What ship is this?"

"The Confederate cruiser *Tallahassee*," Wood replied.

The pilot turned pale, but quickly braced himself and made the best of his plight. The pilot boat proved to be the *James Funk*, one of a class of sturdy schooners stationed between 100 and 200 miles outside New York harbor.

The *Tallahassee* escaping Wilmington

Century Magazine

A prize crew of two officers and twenty men were placed aboard the *James Funk* and she proved to be productive in capturing other vessels and in leading them to the *Tallahassee*, where the former cavalry officer determined their fate. Soon there were more than forty prisoners and their baggage cluttering the deck.

When the *James Funk* brought the newly captured schooner *Carroll* alongside, Wood decided to put her in bond and and use her to send his prisoners ashore in New York. All the captives were paroled before they boarded the *Carroll*. One Union captain told Wood he would be reconciled to his vessel's loss if his parole would protect him from the draft.

The black-hulled cruiser's next capture was another pilot boat, the *William Bell*. Wood's objective in capturing pilot boats was to procure a pilot who could either be bribed or coerced to navigate his cruiser through New York harbor's Hell Gate into Long Island Sound. It was his intention to race up the East River just after dark, setting fire to shipping on both sides of the river and then to shell the Brooklyn Navy Yard, hoping to set fire to the buildings and dockside naval vessels. Finally, he would dash through the Hell Gate into Long Island Sound.

From the daily papers he obtained from captured vessels, Wood learned what vessels were currently in New York harbor and thus realized there were no armed vessels ready to interfere with his planned thrust into the commercial center of the Union. However, he never found a pilot who could be bribed or who was disposed to assist him and Wood had to abandon his plan.

It was just as well that he did forego his bold plan. On August 12, Gideon Welles, Union Secretary of the Navy, became aware the *Tallahassee* was operating off New York. Shortly, sixteen vessels were searching for the elusive Confederate raider.

Wood spent three days steaming between the *New York Light Ship* and Montauk Point, sometimes coming within thirty miles of the former. During that period he and his tender seized twenty more vessels. The largest of these was the the thousand- ton packet *Adriatic*, inbound from London with 170 passengers and a valuable cargo. Shortly after this capture,

Century Magazine

The burning of the *Suliote*

Wood's tender, the former *James Funk*, arrived alongside with a recent captured bark, the *Suliote*.

Saddled with many more prisoners than he could handle, Wood decided to send them ashore in the bark. It took three hours to transfer the *Adriatic's* passengers to the *Suliote*. In many cases the passengers, mostly German immigrants, insisted upon taking broken china, bird cages, straw beds and other useless articles, leaving their valuables behind.

Once they were safely aboard the *Suliote*, the *Adriatic* was fired. As the summer evening darkened, the burning ship illuminated the ocean for miles. The *Tallahassee*, having exhausted the bountiful New York hunting grounds, steamed slowing eastward toward Nantucket, towing the *James Funk* in her wake.

The tender soon proved to be incapable of any rapid movement and was destroyed off Nantucket as the *Tallahassee* rounded South Shoal Lightship and prowled towards Boston Bay. The cruiser did sight a few sails and made several unimportant captures before the *Glenarvon*, a new vessel from Thomaston, Maine, inbound from Glasgow with a cargo of iron, was run down and captured.

The *Glenarvon's* captain and his wife were aboard, as were another captain and his wife, who were returning to the United States as passangers. Wood ordered the vessel scuttled and Captain Watts and his wife stood and watched, tears in their eyes, as their home sank into the depths.

Mrs. Watts, shortly afterwards, remarked about her husband: "Poor fellow, he has been going to sea for thirty years, and all of our savings were in that ship. We were saving for our dear children at home — five of them."

Praising Mrs. Watts in his *Century Magazine* article, Woods wrote:

> Miserable business is war, ashore or afloat. A brave, true, and gentle woman, at the same time strong in her conviction of what she thought was right, was the captain's wife, and she soon won the admiration and respect of all on board. But what shall we say of the passenger and his wife? ... She came on board scolding and left scolding. Her tongue was slung amidships, and never tired. Her poor husband, patient and meek as a patriach, came in for his full share. ... At rare intervals there was a calm and then she employed the time in distributing tracts and Testaments.

Century Magazine

The sinking of the *Glenarvon*

Wood soon put the disguntled woman and her husband on a passing Russian ship. The woman continued to lash Wood and his crew with her tongue as she left the *Tallahassee*. In a final grand gesture she snatched her bonnet off her head, tore it into pieces and threw it into the sea.

The *Tallahassee* ran along the Maine coast as far as Matinicus Island, at the entrance to Penobscot Bay, where people on shore could be seen watching the Confederate's passage. Running in and out of seasonal fog banks, Wood raised havoc with the local fishing fleet and coastal traffic. Hundreds of miles from Wilmington, the *Tallahassee* was beginning to run low on coal.

Ashore, the press was reporting the Tallahassee's destructive passage along the coast. The Machias *Republican* commented on September 1, 1864:

THE REBEL PIRATE TALLAHASSEE

> This villanous pirate is reported as making havoc among our fishermen on the eastern coast, and we fear there is much truth in it. The fishermen are as plentiful as blackberries and she would have nothing to do but run in among and burn them. If Uncle Sam would let the job of catching this pirate, as well as others, to the lowest bidder, with the promise of the vessel to boot, she would be taken in three days.

Steering around Cape Sable Island, the western extremity of Nova Scotia, Wood overhauled and captured the *James Littlefield* of Bangor, Maine, inbound from Cardiff, Wales for New York with a cargo of coal. A strong sea and almost constant fogs made it impossible for Wood's crew to transfer the vital coal from the *James Littlefield*. Wood considered accomplishing the transfer in a secluded Nova Scotia harbor, but realized such an operation would be a clear case of the violation of neutral territory. Regretfully, Wood ordered the coal- carrying vessel scuttled.

The *Tallahassee* haunted the sea lanes off the Maine and Nova Scotia coasts for three days, darting in and out of the ever-present fog banks, without sighting another vessel.

Probing the fog, searching for the Nova Scotia coastline and a neutral port, the Confederate raider came upon a red-headed fisherman in small boat almost under the *Tallahassee's* bow. The fisherman bellowed a warning about not tearing his nets and then softened his attitude and offered to pilot the *Tallahassee* into a safe port. Taking the small boat in tow, Wood accepted the red-head's offer. Soon the *Tallahassee* emerged from the fog to find the city of Halifax dead ahead.

Coming to anchor, Wood had his gig brought alongside and left to pay courtesy calls on Sir James Hope, commander of *H.M.S. Duncan* and of the Halifax Naval Station, and on Lieutenant Governor Richard Graves MacDonnell. Wood found Hope rather cold and unfriendly, while MacDonnell was definately more cordial. However, the latter did remind the Confederate captain that under the terms of the Queen's Neutrality Proclamation, belligerents could only remain in port for twenty-fours hours and could only load enough coal to enable the them to reach the nearest home port.

The *Tallahassee* had damaged a spar when she collided with the *Adriatic* off New York. Wood appealed for additional time to repair the damaged spar and MacDonnell granted him an additional twelve hours to replace it.

Wood had arrived in Halifax with only forty tons of coal remaining in in his bunkers. Governor MacDonnell ruled that the raider could load 100 tons in Halifax and the work of loading soon began while the cruiser lay docked at the harbor's Woodside district. Benjamin Weir, the resident Confederate agent in Halifax, secured a supply of coal from the Prussian bark *Marie Griefswold*.

US Consul Mortimer M. Jackson, well aware that Union gunboats were searching for the *Tallahassee*, brought pressure on both MacDonnell and Hope to prevent Wood from loading more coal than necessary to reach a southern port. Spurred on by Jackson, Hope sent an officer aboard to observe the coal transfer and surrounded the *Tallahassee* with eleven armed boats. Wood protested the British action, and MacDonnell ordered the mini-blockade raised, but reminded the Confederate he could load no more than 100 tons. Actually, Wood was able to load a total of 120 tons, twenty tons more than the British decision allowed.

Maritime Museum of the Atlantic, Halifax

The C.S.S. *Tallahassee* in Halifax Harbor.

Apparently, the departure of the British boats allowed a few of the *Tallahassee's* crew to jump ship. The Halifax *Express* reported:

> Since the arrival in port of the Confederate Steamer *Tallahassee,* a number of desertions from the vessel have taken place. Some of them have been arrested and confined at the Police Station, awaiting the orders of the officers of the ships.

The pro-Confederate Halifax *Citizen,* commenting on the rules under which the *Tallahasee* was allowed to re-coal, noted:

> ... When it is remembered that the Union war steamers that came in here last winter in search of the *Chesapeake* were allowed to remain as long as they pleased, and to take in what coal they wanted, it appears to be rather one-sided neutrality to treat this Confederate ship with such a rigid reading of "the law."

Wood, reading the local and New York newspaper reports of his ship's successful cruise, was aware that Union Secretary of the Navy Gideon Welles had a large number of vessels searching for the *Tallahassee.* He was also aware of the danger of having to run out of Halifax to the open sea through a gauntlet of Union warships. In fact, the *U.S.S. Pontoosuc* was already steaming from Eastport, Maine to Halifax to prevent the Confederate cruiser's departure.[*]

A new spar was secured and brought aboard, but was stowed, rather than being stepped in place. The coaling operation was stopped and Wood asked Benjamin Weir to secure a good pilot to guide the sea-ready *Tallahassee* out of Halifax's harbor.

Soon harbor pilot Jock Fleming was climbing aboard and assuring Wood he could take the raider to sea, avoiding any Union gunboats hovering around the passage to deep water.

Years later, in his *Century Magazine* article, Wood wrote a wonderful description of Fleming:

> He was six feet in height, broad, deep-chested, and with a stoop. His limbs were too long for his body. His head was

---

[*]Eleven other vessels were ranging the Eastern seaboard searching for the *Tallahassee.* They were: *Juniata, Susquehanna, Eolus, Dunbarton, Tristram Shandy, Moccasin, Aster, Yantic, R. R. Cuyler, Grand Gulf, Dacotah* and *San Jacinto.*

pitched well forward, and covered, as was his neck, with a thick
stubble of grayish hair. His eyes were small and bright, almost
hid beneath overhanging eyebrows. His hands were as hard,
rough, and scaly as the flipper of a green turtle. ... He knew the
harbor as well as the fish that swam its waters. He was honest,
bluff, and trusty.

Halifax's harbor is divided by McNab's Island, creating two
channels to the sea. The western, or main passage, is deep,
broad and straight. The eastern passage, used only by small
coastal vessels, is narrow, shallow, and, at that time, un-
marked by lights or buoys. At low water its shallowest point
was only covered by a fathom or less of water.

Fleming assured Wood he could take the *Tallahassee* out
through the eastern passage, but was worried about the larger
ships' ability to "turn the corner." Wood guaranteed his ship,
because it had twin-screw propellers, could turn around on
her center.

At midnight, August 19, 1864, the *Tallahassee* hove her
anchor and started to sea. Soon dark clouds, sweeping across
the sky from the south, obscured the waning moon. Steaming
slowly, the ship's crew could just make out the dark shore of
McNab's Island on one side and the mainland on the other. A
small boat, with a dim light showing, was sent ahead to mark
sharp turns in the passage.

In an hour Wood saw the beacon of the lighthouse on
Devil's Island and the channel deepened and widened. Soon
the swells of the Atlantic could be felt under the hull and the
Tallahassee was safely outside the passage, leaving the
gathering Union forces far to the westward. The *Pontoosuc*
actually arrived off Halifax four hours after the *Tallahassee*
made her escape. Fleming's small boat was dropped
alongside and the master pilot and his pitching craft soon
disappeared in the darkness.

The *Tallahassee's* run down the coast was uneventful. She
captured and burned the brig *Roan,* her only victim on her
return home. Wood decided to avoid Bermuda, where he had
hoped to re-coal, because of the prevalence of yellow fever on
the island. On August 25th, six days after he slipped out of
Halifax, John Taylor Wood successfully ran the blockade into
Wilmington, after being chased and fired upon by several
Union ships.

Nova Scotia Provincial Archives
Jock Fleming, Halifax Harbor Pilot

The *Tallahassee* later made one more short cruise under another captain and was then seized by the authorities in Liverpool, England. Handed over to the United States government, she was later sold to the Japanese as a merchant brig.*

The *Florida*, also named by Jones as one of the vessels to be used in the Maine expedition, left Brest, France on February 10, 1864 and stopped in Bermuda several months later. There, her commander, Lieutenant Charles M. Morris, received instructions to attack shipping along the New England coast. Enroute to New England waters, the Confederate ship tangled with the *America*, a Union steam tug, which eluded her and ran into New York to warn Secretary of the Navy Gideon Welles the *Florida* was close enough to shore to chase and capture.

On July 9, 1864, a little more than a week before William Collins's ill-fated raid on the Calais Bank, the Florida captured and burned the bark *General Berry* thirty-five miles off Maryland's eastern shore. That same day the *Florida* captured another four more vessels in the same general area. Realizing Union ships would soon be searching for him, Morris turned the *Florida* eastward, seeking sanctuary deep in the Atlantic.

On July 18th, the very day the Confederate raiders attempted to raid the Calais Bank, Governor Samuel Cony of Maine wrote Secretary of the Navy Welles about the *Florida's* bold actions off the east coast. In his letter he asked that several gunboats be assigned to patrol the coast and then wrote:

> We are at war with a brave, energetic adversary, fruitful in resources, ready to strike at any exposed point, and which, with one or two piratical cruisers, besides destroying a great amount of tonnage, has driven a large share of our commerce under the protection of flags of other nations.

Fleeing for the safety of the Canary Islands, the *Florida* abandoned the rewarding East Coast raiding grounds. On October 7th, while the Calais bank raiders were on trial in the Machias court, the *C.S.S. Florida* was captured in the neutral harbor of Bahia, Brazil by the *U. S. S. Wachusett*.

---

*Re-named the *Haya Maro*, she was shipwrecked on July 17, 1869 on a voyage From Yokohama to Kobe.

CHAPTER SEVEN

TRIAL, PRISON AND A DARING ESCAPE

The case of the Calais bank robbers was presented to the Supreme Judicial Court, which met in Machias in October of 1864. The presiding judge was Charles Danforth of Gardiner. William Daymond, Consul Howard's informer, was on hand to testify against his fellow bank raiders. Their case was first taken under advisement and for a time it appeared they would have to be treated as prisoners of war, rather than as common criminals. However, they were ultimately found guilty of conspiring to rob the Calais Bank and were sentenced to three years' confinement at the Maine State Prison in Thomaston.

The press coverage of the trial was meager and confined to reporting that a trial had been held and that the trio had been sentenced to the prison at Thomaston. The few records pertaining to the trial, which are now in the collections of the Maine State Archives in Augusta, consist of a copy of the raiders' indictment, a bare-boned summary of the Court's actions during the trial and a copy of the bill for the trial. Since the trial was held before the day of the court reporter, there is apparently no verbatim record in existence.

The best contemporary report of the trial is found in a letter written by William Collins, shortly after the trial. From his cell he wrote:

State Prison Thomaston
October 23, 1864

My Dear Sister

I have been sentenced to this place for a term of three years. I will give you some particulars of the trial, (if so it may be called), We refused to plead before a civil tribunal, for invading their state, and attempting acts of hostility under our proper flag. They would not acknowledge us, as Confederates, and we would not acknowledge them, or their rights, to try us by a civil court.(and made no defense)

But to speak of the evidence, it was false and contradictory, the witnesses made no scruples about perjuring themselves; one of the principle of who one, was an avowed infidel. The Judge himself was so much satisfied of it, that in his charge to the jury, he stated that it was not necessary to prove that an attempt had been made, but that a conspiracy had been formed, for some undefined object. He thought such a conspiracy had been formed and as for being Confederates he acknowledged no such Authority, (though he was perfectly satisfied that we were acting under lawful authority), and he also stated to the jury, an unqualified falsehood, as the Prosecuting Attorney acknowledged, the next day when he came down to try, and make his peace with us for he was not easy in his mind about the future.

It was this that it was not lawful for a belligerent, to destroy the private property of his enemy. Ships are private property, yet are lawfully destroyed, I am a Naval Officer, therefore can destroy such. They offered to swear us as evidence in our own defense, but we would not be sworn, or we could have easily disproved, the principle part of the evidence, but it would have given them information which it would not been right for them to have.

The charge of robbery, that even there (sic) own witness was compelled to state was never once mentioned, He acknowledged we were Confederates and that we unfurled our flag on the hights (sic) behind the city.

As to our intentions I have never denied them and they are thus all Confederate soldiers may do against an enemy with whom we are at war in a lawful manner. Write to me and let me know anything that might interest me. I remain your affectionate brother

Wm

Maine State Archives

The bill for the Calais Bank Raiders trial.

A short note, written after the letter was completed, appears at the top of the first page. It says: "If you receive an answer from Richmond Va you need not send it to me. I send you two Pounds to use as you please for postage etc. We are all quite well and expect to get along very well until exchanged Which I hope will be soon."

It is interesting that Collins was apparently expecting an answer from Richmond regarding his previous requests that Confederate authorities be notified of his capture. He could not have known that in August Secretary of the Navy Stephen R. Mallory had written an interesting letter regarding his case to the Mississippi Adjutant General in Macon, Mississippi.

> Confederate States of America
> Navy Department
> Richmond, August 27, 1864
>
> Col. W. H. McCardle
> Adj Gen
> Macon, Mipi (sic)
> Your letter of the 16th inst. enclosing Acting Master William Collins' commission in the Navy and calling attention to his case has been received and the commission is herewith returned.
> I have called the attention of Col. Ould, our agent of exchange, to Wm Collins' case and requested him to [three indecipherable words] the list of our Naval officers to be exchanged and to call the attention of the Federal authorities to the fact that he is an officer of the Navy.
> I am respectfully
> S R Mallory
> Secretary of The Navy

Nothing apparently ever came from the Secretary's efforts on Collins' behalf, but they must be considered highly significant in considering Collins' claims of legitimacy.

Their trial completed and sentence having been passed, the raiders were transported to Thomaston by wagon and steamboat. Passing through the coastal town of Ellsworth, the convicted conspirators hurrahed for Jefferson Davis. In Bangor, where they boarded the steamer *Katahdin* for the trip to Thomaston, they told a large dock-side crowd they would be freed as soon as President Davis demanded their release.

Collins, still boasting, said they had been sent to Calais on regular Confederate service and that they would have been successful in their mission if it had not been for treachery.

The Confederates' post-trial predictions of an early release proved wrong for two of the raiders. However, the boastful William Collins, who was assigned to work in the prison carriage shop, served only thirty-six days of his sentence before he had had enough of his new home.

On November 26, 1864, just after the rising bell, Collins, along with four other convicts, left the carriage shop and ran to one of the guard posts, where they began to throw stones at the guard. They hit him hard with their first missiles and followed with more volleys. Ripping a pair of steps away from the shoe shop, they flung them against the wall. Collins ran up the steps first, hurled a guard aside, and jumped over the wall. The others quickly followed.

The guards fired three shots at the fleeing prisoners and succeeded in capturing one. Another of the escapees, who broke his leg going over the wall, was found hiding in a nearby lime kiln.

Collins and the others commenced to swim the frigid St. George River, which ran near the prison. One man drowned, but Collins and William Devine made it to the far shore. Devine, exhausted and chilled, stopped at a house to warm up. He was detained by the lady living there, until officers from the prison could arrive to arrest him.

Collins crawled under a log as prison guards searched the woods. At one point, according to Reverend John Collins, who wrote about the incident in later life, a guard actually stood on top of a log under which William was hiding.

As soon as it was dark and the guards returned to the prison. Collins, leaving the shelter of his log, set out again until he finally stopped at the house of William Kolleran in Cushing. The escaping raider rapped on the door and a voice from inside asked who was there. Collins replied, " A friend." When the door was opened, the escapee, still dressed in his prison garb, entered and demanded protection.

Mr. Kolleran, who had heard about Collins and the Calais bank raiders did not want to harbor the escapee, but Mrs. Kolleran, who saw the intruder was shaking with cold, said she would take a chance as it was "inhuman not to warm and feed a man in such condition."

Sally G. Hill

The Maine State Prison shortly after the Civil War.

Early the next morning Collins left the Kolleran's house. He tried to give Mrs. Kolleran the 75¢ he had in his pocket, but she refused payment. Climbing high up a tall pine tree, overlooking Broad Cove on the St. George River, he watched prison officers search the countryside for him.

That night he stole a dory and crossed the river. On the other side he stopped at a farm, where the farmer gave him breakfast.

Meanwhile, back at the prison, Warden Rice offered a $50 reward for Collins' capture, which led the Portland *Transcript* to comment, "That won't fetch the rascal!" Another paper, reporting Collins had been seen in Cushing said, "... he ought to be shot on sight."

As a result of this escape, the prison guards were armed with new Spencer rifles, capable of firing fifteen rounds in rapid succession, and were given an additional fifteen rounds to carry in their pockets.

In a letter reporting Collins' escape to Consul Howard in St. John, Warden Rice wrote, "Governor Cony is very desirous that he should be arrested ... and will be glad to pay whatever expense ... beside the reward that the statute allows me to offer." Reminding Howard that Collins' family lived near St. John, the warden asked the consul to "take some pains to have him arrested."

Warden Rice was correct when he predicted Collins would head for St. John. On the evening of January 2, 1865 a man walked into St. Stephens, New Brunswick, across the St. Croix River from Calais. Questioned, he freely admitted he was William Collins, the Calais Bank raider and an escapee from the Maine State Prison. The next morning he left on foot for St. John.

In an effort to escape the watchful eye of detectives and informers in St. John he obtained an old cowhide coat and a pair of moccasins, which disguised him so thoroughly that even his friends failed to recognize him. His sister Mary, who had not agreed with either his views or his mission, welcomed him to the family home in Loch Lomand, where he spent the night. The next morning he boarded a ship for Halifax, where he transferred to another ship bound for the South.

Little accurate information is available regarding Collins's actions after he returned to the Confederacy. However, records in the National Archives do indicate he was paroled by the Federal authorities in Grenada, Mississippi on May 18, 1865.

Jones and Phillips were still incarcerated at Thomaston. At the state capitol in Augusta, Governor Samuel Cony and the Executive Council were bombarded with pardon petitions on behalf of young Francis X. Jones from prominent citizens of St. Louis. The petitioners included Marshall Brotherton, Judge of the County Court and President of the Bremen Savings Bank; and Peter L. Foy, Postmaster.

All of the petitions stressed young Jones was the sole support of his poor, invalid mother, "a good Union woman"; and a young man whom the "wicked rebellion" brought "under the baneful influences of associates to whom he owes all the calamities which have befallen him and which visit his mother, now in old age, with so much distress."

Governor Cony and the Executive Council granted a full pardon for his part in the Calais bank raid to Francis X. Jones on January 15, 1866.

With Jones on his way back to his mother in St. Louis, William Phillips was the last of the raiders still in prison. Writing to the Governor Cony on May 1, 1866, Phillips reminded him that he had been confined for a crime committed during wartime, while under the command of an officer of the Confederate States of America.

Closing his appeal, he said, "I would humbly beg you to grant me a pardon that I may once more start out into the world determined as I am to live an honest and upright life."

After considering Phillips' case, the Governor and his Council pardoned Phillips on May 7, 1866 and the last of the Calais Bank raiders left Maine.

However, William Collins, always a bold man, returned to the Pine Tree State again. Ten years after the war he visited Reverend John Collins, who was then the pastor of a church in Fryeburg, a small community on the South-western Maine-New Hampshire border.

Anxious to know whether his brother knew who had first put the authorities on his track, the Reverend asked the

David G.Engel

The author, left, and Earle G. Shettleworth, director of the Maine Historical Preservation Commission, with William Collins' Confederate regimental flag, which was presented to the Maine Historical Society by Reverend John Collins.

former Confederate, "Do you know who betrayed you to the United States authorities?"

"No," the Calais Bank raider replied, as he drew a revolver from his pocket. "If I did I should loan him what lead there is in this gun. And I should do it so quickly that he wouldn't have time to say his prayers." Relating the episode to a congregation years later, Reverend Collins exclaimed, "I didn't care to tell him all I knew about it."

This is the way Reverend Collins told the story in later years. William might not have known that his own brother had a part in his capture, but he certainly knew the part undercover agent William Daymond had played in his arrest.

When William Collins left St. John for the South after his escape from the Maine State Prison in Thomaston, he left behind the blue and gold flag of his old regiment, the 15th Mississippi.

Later, Reverend John Collins brought the flag to Maine and in 1912 he presented it to the Maine Historical Society in Portland.

Today, visitors to the Society may see this flag in the Society's museum. It is a tangible reminder of the Confederate raid on the Calais Bank.

CHAPTER EIGHT

CHARLES W. READ, CSN & THE FLORIDA NO. 2

William Collins, Francis X. Jones and William Phillips were not the first Confederates to find themselves behind bars in Maine. In June of 1863, a year previously, a group of Confederates had been incarcerated at Fort Preble in South Portland. They had been captured after they had entered Portland harbor and had stolen the U.S. Revenue Cutter *Caleb Cushing* from its mooring early on the morning of June 27th.

This fearless expedition into the inner harbor of Maine's largest city was led by Lieutenant Charles William Read, CSN. Read, twenty-three years old at the time of the Portland raid, had graduated from the U.S. Naval Academy at Annapolis, Maryland, in 1860 at the bottom of his class of twenty-five men.

The Raymond, Mississippi native joined the Confederate Navy when the Civil War broke out and was posted to the C.S.S. *McRae*. Read's first naval assignment, formerly the Mexican screw bark *Marques de la Habana*, was assigned to defend the lower Mississippi River and to protect blockade runners sliding in and out of Mobile Bay and the Mississippi River.

The *McRae's* crew distinguished themselves during a spirited engagement at the Head of the Mississippi River Passes on October 12, 1861 and had their ship cut to ribbons in the defense of Forts Jackson and Philip on April 24, 1862.

U.S. Navy

Charles W. Read, wearing the uniform of a midshipman at Annapolis.

The *McRae* was hopelessly out-gunned in skirmishes with several Union warships during defense of these forts. The crew were left dead and dying on the bloody decks. Lt. Thomas B. Huger, the *McRae's* commander, was mortally wounded.

Young Charles W. Read assumed command of the stricken ship, which was completely riddled by Union fire, and maneuvered her up river to New Orleans under a flag of truce. Abandoned by Read and the remaining crew, the *McRae* was found sunk alongside the city wharf by Union forces the following day.

Read was commissioned a 2nd Lieutenant on October 23, 1862 and assigned to the C.S.S. *Florida*, then commanded by Captain John Newland Maffitt, a daring sea devil of the Confederacy. Writing in his journal about Read on the day of the latter's arrival aboard the *Florida*, Maffitt said: "Mr. Read is quiet and slow, and not much of a military officer of the deck, but I think him reliable and sure, though slow." Later, Maffitt changed his opinion of young Read and wrote: "Daring beyond the point of martial prudence." The *Florida* was being outfitted in Mobile, Alabama when Read joined her. Having taken aboard the stores and the gun accessories she needed, along with additional crew members, the *Florida* set sail for the high seas on January 16,1863. She re-coaled at Nassau in the Bahamas, and then spent six months capturing and destroying Union shipping off the coasts of North and South America and in the West Indies.

On May 6, 1863, off Cape St. Roque, Brazil, the *Florida* captured the brigantine *Clarence*, which was bound from Rio de Janeiro to Baltimore, Maryland with a cargo of coffee. Young Charles Read saw the newly captured *Clarence* as an opportunity to slash through the Union blockade and attack the Federal naval force at Hampton Roads, Virginia. In a formal request to Captain Maffitt, Read wrote:

> I propose to take the brig which we have just captured, and with a crew of twenty men, to proceed to Hampton Roads and cut out a gunboat or steamer of the enemy.

> As I would be in possession of the brig's papers, and as the crew would not be large enough to excite suspicion, there can be no doubt of my passing Fortress Monroe successfully. Once in the Roads I would be prepared to avail myself of any circumstance which might present for gaining the deck of an enemy's vessel. If it was found impossible to board a gunboat or merchant steamer, it would be possible to fire the shipping at Baltimore.

Read also requested he be allowed to take Eugene H. Brown, 3rd assistant engineer of the *Florida*, and a fireman with him on the *Clarence*.

Captain Maffitt replied on the same day, giving his permission, and suggested:

> ... you may meet with success by centering your views upon Hampton Roads. The *Sumpter* (a Cromwell steamer) is now a kind of flagship anchored off Hampton Bay, and at midnight might be carried by boarding. If you find that impracticable, the large quantity of shipping at the fort, or in Norfolk, could be fired, and you and your crew escape to Burwell's Bay, thence making your way safely to Confederate lines.
>
> The proposition evinces on your part patriotic devotion to the cause of your country, and this is certainly the time when all our best exertions should be made to harm the common enemy and confuse them with attacks from unexpected quarters. I agree with your request and will not hamper you with instructions.
>
> Act for the best, and God speed you. ...

Captain Maffitt provided Read and the *Clarence* with a 12-pound howitzer and ammunition, six rifles, thirteen revolvers and ten pistols. At 4 p. m., May 6, 1863, the *Clarence* was put into commission as the *Florida No. 2*. Read and the *Clarence* headed north and the *Florida* continued to hunt Union shipping off the Brazilian coast.

A month later, June 6, 1863, Read captured his first prize, the *Whistling Wind*, in the Atlantic east of Cape Romain, South Carolina. Read burned the bark and her $14,000 cargo of coal destined for the U.S. Navy. On the following day he captured and bonded the *Alfred H. Partridge*, bound from New York for Matamoras, Mexico with a cargo of arms and clothing.

Two days later Read captured and burned the brig *Mary Alvina*, bound from Boston to New Orleans with a cargo of commissary stores. After interrogating prisoners from the

Mary Alvina, Read decided it would be too difficult to try and force a passage through the Union Navy to enter Hampton Roads.

In a later report to Stephen R. Mallory, Confederate Secretary of the Navy, Read wrote:

> No vessels were allowed to go into Hampton Roads unless they had supplies for the U.S. Government, and then they were closely watched. The vessels lying at the wharf above Fortress Monroe were guarded by gunboats, and there were sentries on the wharf. Just outside the fort there were two boarding steamers. I then determined to cruise along the coast and try and intercept a transport for Fortress Monroe and with her endeavor to carry out the orders of Commander Maffitt, and in the meantime to do all possible injury to the enemy's commerce.

On June 12th, at 9 o'clock in the morning, Captain William G. Munday of the *Tacony* was almost in sight of Cape Henry, when he noticed a brig with the United States flag flying upside down. At first he was hesitant, but when he saw men who were in apparent distress, he turned the *Tacony* and headed toward the other vessel.

The brig, which of course was the *Clarence*, launched a small boat to meet the *Tacony*. Read's men, all in seamen's uniforms, clambered aboard the *Tacony*, where they quickly flashed hidden weapons and took the entire *Tacony* crew prisoner, transferring them to the *Clarence*.

Shortly after he captured the *Tacony*, Read seized the *M. A. Shindler*, bound from Port Royal to Philadelphia in ballast, using the same "upside-down flag" ruse.

Read concluded the *Tacony* was a faster and better vessel than the *Clarence* and decided to continue his marauding cruise aboard the former vessel. The Confederate crew was in the process of putting their lone howitzer aboard the *Tacony* when another schooner, the *Kate Stewart* from Key West to Philadelphia, came into view.

Read had been caught pants down! His howitzer was temporarily out of action. The new arrival was drawing closer. Aboard the *Clarence*, a section of spar, intended to resemble a howitzer, was hastily pointed over the side and the *Kate*

Stewart was hailed and ordered to heave to. The "Quaker gun" did the trick and the schooner became the third prize of the day.

Read then burned both the *Clarence* and the *M. A. Schindler* and started after a fourth vessel, the brig *Arabella*, which he soon overhauled. The *Arabella* was carrying neutral cargo and Read released her in $30,000 bond.

However, Read had a small problem. His provisions were running low and he was saddled with over fifty prisoners. He decided to bond the *Kate Stewart* and send his prisoners ashore aboard her.

In a week's time, Read and his crew had captured six vessels .... four in a single day.

Captain Munday, formerly commander of the *Tacony*, stepped ashore from the *Kate Stewart* in Philadelphia at 3 P. M. the next day. One hour and twenty-five minutes later the Navy Department in Washington, D. C. received the following telegram:

> The pirate *Clarence* captured, within sight of Cape Henry, yesterday morning, brig *Schindler* and schooner *Kate Stewart* and bark *Tacony*, of this port. They are using the *Tacony* for pirating further.
>
> E. A. Souder & Co.

That same day E.A. Souder & Co., a firm of Philadelphia merchants, followed up their telegram with a letter to Gideon Welles, Union Secretary of the Navy. The letter concluded by urging the Secretary to take prompt action to capture the *Tacony* because:

> The crew [of the *Clarence*] told Captain Munday that the *Clarence*, the day before, was pursued by a United States gunboat and threw overboard their guns, except a small swivel, and consequently they have no armament on board the bark *Tacony* and could be captured readily in forty-eight hours if a steamer with a single gun was sent after her, or a sailing vessel in disguise.

Welles moved fast!. He ordered Rear-Admiral Samuel P. Lee at Newport News, Virginia to "Send out anything you have available." Similar telegrams were sent to the commanders of the Boston, Philadelphia and New York Navy Yards. The chase was on!

By midnight the steamers *Young Rover*, *Commodore Jones* and *Western World* had sailed from Hampton Roads in search of the *Tacony*. On the following day the *Seminole*, *Tuscarora*, *Dai Ching*, *Adela* and *Virginia*, all steamers, left the New York Navy Yard hunting for Read and the *Tacony*. Many other vessels, both naval ships and chartered craft, followed suit on the 15th and 16th.

Three chartered steamers left Philadelphia on the 15th and the next day a fourth one joined them in pursuit of the *Tacony*. On the same day, five chartered vessels sailed from Boston to search New England waters. On the 17th, the steamer *Montgomery* and the bark *Trinity* left Boston to join the chase. The steamer *Cherokee* also left at the same time, but had to return to port to have a faulty compass repaired. She sailed again twenty-four hours later.

Many of the vessels were sent to sea under the command of junior officers; however, their quarry, Second Lieutenant Charles W. Read, CSN, was himself a young officer of only twenty-three years.

The *Suwanee* was commanded by Acting Ensign G. W. Corner. The *Kate Stewart*, captured and bonded by Read on June 12th, was sent to sea again under the command of Acting Master John West. The *Adela* was commanded by L. N. Stodder, who held the unusual rank of Acting Volunteer Lieutenant.

In many cases the vessels' crews were hastily assembled. In Philadelphia, day laborers, who were also seamen, were used to man chartered vessels, rather than utilize enlisted naval personnel.

Many of the ships sent to sea in search of Read were in poor shape. The *Dai Ching*, commanded by Lt.-Commander J. C. Chaplin, was incapable of making more than five and a half knots. Chaplin reported to the Navy Department: "I boarded no vessels, being unable, from the slowness of this vessel, to overhaul them under the most favorable circumstances."

The *Seminole*, capable of making eleven knots, spent seven days at sea searching for the *Tacony* along the inner edge of the Gulf Stream off the Virginia Capes.

During that time she never had less than fourteen inches of water inside her hull and three donkey pumps, working continually, could not control the water's flow. The cause was traced to uncaulked planking in the upper works where the water was leaking aboard at a rate of five to six inches an hour.

The yacht *America*, manned by midshipmen from the U. S. Naval Academy, logged ten days at sea searching for the *Tacony*. Her first five days were spent in stormy, wet foggy weather fighting easterly winds. The yacht's jib shackle carried away at the cutwater*   in a heavy sea late in the afternoon of her third day at sea. Lt. Theodore F. Kane, commanding, feared he would lose the foremast in the weather, since the jib stay was the foremast's only fore-and-aft support.

Crippled, the *America* kept close to shore and turned back to New York after reaching the Chesapeake capes.

At least one Union skipper resorted to a ruse in searching for the *Tacony*. The *Kate Stewart*, herself hunting for her former captor, was stopped and boarded by the crew of the *Adela*. The *Adela* then lowered her American flag and raised an English flag to her peak and sailed off on a southerly course in search of the *Tacony*.

Read and the *Tacony*, in spite of their pursuers, continued to harass, capture, burn and destroy Union shipping. Between June 12th and June 24 they captured fifteen vessels.

On the 15th, off the Virginia coast, Read subjugated and burned the brig *Umpire*, which was carrying a cargo of sugar and molasses from Cardenas to Boston.

On the 20th the *Tacony* captured the ship *Isaac Webb*, bound from Liverpool to New York. The *Webb* carried more than 750 passengers and Read, unable to handle such a large number of prisoners, bonded her for $40,000. Later in the same day he seized and torched the *Micawber*, a fishing schooner.

Shortly thereafter Confederate crew member Robert Muller was put in irons for saying he "... wished a Yankee gunboat would come alongside and take us."

On the 21st Read captured and set fire to the clipper ship *Byzantium*, enroute from London to New York with a load of coal. Three crew members from the *Byzantium* elected to join Read aboard the *Tacony* as members of the Confederate vessel's marauding crew.

---

*Fore part of a ship's prow

Harper's Weekly

The *Tacony* burning vessels along the Eastern seaboard.

That afternoon Read captured and sank the bark *Goodspeed*, which was travelling from Londonderry to New York in ballast.

On the 22nd, off the New England coast, the young Confederate raider added the vessels *Marengo*, *Florence*, the *Elizabeth Ann* and *Ripple*, all fishing schooners, to his list of prizes. The *Florence* was an old vessel, and Read bonded her and placed seventy-five prisoners aboard. He then burned the other three schooners.

About 4 A.M. on June 23rd, Read fooled a Federal vessel, which was searching for him, and cleverly escaped the tightening Union dragnet.

The *Tacony* lay becalmed 45 miles off the entrance to Portland (Maine) Harbor, according to Robert Hunt, one of the sailors from the *Byzantium* who had joined Read's crew, when the lookout reported a steamer ahead. Read hurried up from below and scanned the approaching vessel with his binoculars. He immediately realized the steamer was in fact a Union gunboat.

Turning to the crew he said, "Well boys, I guess our frolics about over, but we must try and fool them." Read then ordered most of the crew out of sight below decks.

Soon the Union gunboat was alongside and her skipper was hailing the *Tacony*: "Bark, ahoy, what and where bound?"

Read replied quickly, "Bark *Mary Jane*, from Sagua La Grande, bound for Portland."

The captain of the gunboat proceeded to informed Read a "rebel privateer" was cruising along the coast burning merchant vessels and that he had better keep "a sharp lookout." Read thanked the Union captain for his warning and then watched as the enemy gunboat steamed off in a southerly direction.*

Calling his crew topside, the Confederate captain warned, "Boys, we have had a close call, but we are still on deck. It is getting too hot for us in this latitude; we must change the program."

---

*A careful search of the *Official Records of the Union And Confederate Navies* ... has failed to uncover any report of this incident by a Union gunboat captain.

Later the same day, Read overtook and destroyed the fishing schooners *Ada* and *Wanderer*.

On the next day, June 24, 1863, Read and the *Tacony* made their last two captures. The first was the ship *Shatemuc*, bound from Liverpool to Boston with a large number of emigrants on board. Read bonded her for $150,000:

> C. S. Bark Florida No. 2
> At Sea, June 24th, 1863
>
> Thirty days after the ratification of a treaty of peace between the Confederate States and the United States of America, I, or we, promise to pay to the President of the Confederate States the sum of one hundred and fifty thousand dollars ($150,000) for the release of the Shatemuc and cargo.
>
> John H. Oxnard,
> Master of the Ship Shatemuc

(Seal written with a pen)

Early in the evening Read made his second capture of the day, the fishing schooner *Archer*, whose crew were just sitting down to a fish chowder supper. Captain Robert Snowman of the *Archer* asked the Confederates to join him at the table. Years later, Robert Hunt wrote: "Their captain asked us to join them, and as they had a first class chowder, besides some nice sounds* and tongues cooked as they knew how to cook them, we accepted the invitation."

Read decided the *Tacony* was becoming too well known in New England waters and ordered his crew to transfer*the howitzer, which was completely out of ammunition, aboard

---

*air bladder of a fish

* The Confederates maintained the log of the *Tacony* after her capture. On June 25th the log entry read: " At 9 A.M. removed from the Barque to the Schooner finished at 2 P.M. everybody being on board burnt the Barque Tacony stood to the NW of the wind."

the *Archer*. In his later report to the Confederate Navy Department he wrote:

> As there were a large number of the enemy's gunboats in search of the *Tacony*, and with our howitzer ammunition being all expended, I concluded to destroy the *Tacony*, and with the schooner *Archer* to proceed along the coast with the view of burning the shipping in some exposed harbor, or of cutting out a steamer.

Read burned the *Tacony* and headed toward the Maine coast. Eight miles southeast of Damariscove Island, the *Archer* came upon two fishermen, Albert P. Bibber and Elbridge Titcomb, in a rowboat tending twenty-five trawls.

The Confederates hailed the fishermen and asked them to come alongside. Bibber replied, "I cannot do it." The Confederates again ordered the row boat alongside and told Bibber and Titcomb to cut their trawls. The fishermen still refused to stop fishing.

Frustrated, Read ordered a small boat carrying five Confederates into the water. The Mainers were soon captured and brought aboard the *Archer*, where they were free to wander the decks.

About an hour later Titcomb was summoned to the cabin to be questioned by Read. Shortly afterwards he was returned to the deck and Bibber was taken to the cabin.

Seated, he was questioned by Read about coastal fishing. Then Read's interrogation turned to the war and the latest news. Probing further, the Confederate asked Bibber about the schedules of Maine coastal steamers and patrolling revenue cutters.

Bibber replied he had been fishing for a number of days and had not heard any late news. However, he did tell Read everything he knew about the steamers and their schedules. He also informed Read that the steamer *Chesapeake*, "a staunch, swift vessel", would be in Portland overnight and that the revenue cutter *Caleb Cushing* might also be in the harbor.

Bibber also told Read he had seen a top-sail schooner that morning making for Boothbay Harbor and that he thought it might possibly have been the *Caleb Cushing*.

National Archives

A water-soaked section of the *Tacony's* log, which was maintained by the Confederate's after they captured the bark.

Read got up and left the cabin. Before leaving he told the fisherman, "All I want of you is to take this vessel in and out of Portland."

Read, armed with Bibber's information, had decided to quietly enter Portland harbor and seize both the *Caleb Cushing* and the *Chesapeake*.

CHAPTER NINE

THE SEIZURE OF THE CALEB CUSHING

Portland's harbor defenses appeared insurmountable to a person viewing them from the Marine Observatory atop the city's Munjoy Hill. The main shipping channel was guarded by no less than three granite masonry forts, situated to destroy any invaders with interlocking fields of fire.

The outermost fort in the system was Fort Scammell, located on House Island. Scammell, whose construction was begun in 1808, was supposedly defended by 71 large guns.

Fort Preble was located on the mainland, facing Fort Scammell. Work on this fort also began in 1808 and was completed in 1812. At the time of the Civil War it was enlarged and renovated. The plan of defense called for two fifteen inch, twenty ten-inch, and twenty-two eight-inch guns, as well as ten thirteen-pounders and eight twenty-four pounders.

The final fort in the triple-threat defense system was Fort Gorges, located on Hog Island Ledge at a point where the outer and inner harbors met. Commenced in 1858, this large stone fort, was designed to complete the harbor defenses by guarding the entrance to the inner, or upper, harbor. It was unmanned at the time of the Confederate's entrance into the

Mason Philip Smith

Fort Scammell on House Island in Portland Harbor.

harbor. Although it was stocked with a large amount of ammunition, only eighteen guns had been mounted on the ramparts.

Portland harbor offered a variety of inviting targets for Read and his men. The first of these was the 460-ton, propeller driven steamship *Chesapeake*, which was tied up at a wharf preparing to make her regular run between Portland and New York.

The steamer had been built in Philadelphia in 1863 as the *Totten*. Rebuilt in 1857, she was renamed the *Chesapeake*. Schooner- rigged with a single funnel, she was owned by H. B. Cromwell & Co. of New York.

Another Portland based steamer, the paddle-wheel-driven *Forest City*, which ran between Portland and Boston, was a possible target. However, the *Forest City* was not then in Portland, but was preparing to leave Boston on her regular run downeast. The most inviting quarry was the U.S. Revenue Cutter *Caleb Cushing*. The *Caleb Cushing*, a 100-foot schooner, armed with a single thirty-two pounder amidships and a twelve pounder on the gallant forecastle, was anchored in the middle of the inner harbor opposite the Custom House.

Captain George Clark, her commander, had died unexpectedly the previous day of a heart attack. The vessel was under the temporary command of Lieutenant Dudley Davenport, a Southerner from Savannah, Georgia. The cutter's new commander, Lieutenant James H. Merryman, U.S.R.S., was due to arrive in Portland the next day aboard the *Forest City*. Most of the cutter's officers and the majority of her crew were ashore on leave, and only a duty watch remained aboard.

The Caleb Cushing had been built in Somerset, Massachusetts in 1853 as a merchant vessel. She had been fitted out as a revenue cutter at the beginning of the war, replacing the regular Portland-based cutter, which had been turned over to the Navy and sent South.

The *Caleb Cushing* had not been intended to serve as a fighting ship. Her duties corresponded more closely to those of a policeman than a soldier. She patroled the rugged Maine coast, rendered aid to ships in distress, and maintained the buoys and channel markers. Ordinarily a revenue cutter was unarmed. Because of the possibility of Southern raids on Northern ports and shipping, the *Caleb Cushing* and her sister cutters had been provided with minimum armament.

When the cutter was re-modeled for the Revenue Service eight compartments had been constructed on her berth deck. Seven of these areas had been designed to be provisioned with potatoes, beans, pork, beef and other food supplies. The eighth was constructed to hold six to eight hundred pounds of powder. In addition, a regular magazine had been built in the aft section, adjacent to the Captain's stateroom. Entrance to this magazine was through a door in his stateroom, which was concealed by a mirror.

Some Portland residents did not think the *Caleb Cushing*, which had been patroling the coast searching for the *Tacony*, provided much protection. An unsigned letter appeared in the *Portland Advertiser* the day before Read entered Portland Harbor:

> The Revenue Cutter, *Caleb Cushing* has returned, after twelve hours ineffectual search after the rebel privateer *Tacony* — or Sir John Franklin. She ran short of provisions, and the barnacles were so thick on her bottom that she couldn't sail fast; so she

has returned and anchored as near the old place as Bone Beef Island will allow. It is said, however, that the Treasury Department will at once have the ferry-boats between this city and the Cape furnished with smooth-bore bow-chasers, and that the people of "Pooduck" are therefore safe from the unprincipled Southern Confederacy.

The city of Portland itself offered Read an   inviting target. His plan called for the Confederates to enter the harbor and seize either a steamer or the *Caleb Cushing*. If the forts fired on the Confederates as they left the inner harbor with their prize, Read planned to turn back and shell the city and burn the *U.S.S. Agawam* and *U.S.S Poutoosac*, two new gunboats waiting for engines at Franklin Wharf.

The Confederates, sailing through outer Casco Bay towards Portland Harbor, were in high spirits. One Southerner wrote in his diary:

> Our new vessel sails like the wind but jumps the devil out of countenance, and jammed up here in the head, I feel the motion sensibly in writing. We have been steering all night W. by N. and this morning I made land, it being the first we have seen ... We are now abreast of Portland Light I believe. This morning we took a boat with two men in it; we will keep them but a short time. They say we are about 40 miles from Portland. Would not there be some excitement in Portland now if they but knew that we were so close to them. A steamer would be out for us in a hurry. We are bound for some daredevil expedition.
>
> Whatever it is I know the general impression is that we shall cut out the Cutter laying in the harbor of Portland, and then take a steamer. If we are only successful we shall have some glory and have taken the sails out of some on board the *Florida*. As soon as they hear of our exploits, I bet they will bite their lips, for I think they have fooled themselves good. So much for rivalry and petty malice. ... If successful in the object, both the Government and people of the U.S. will be somewhat astonished. It is a noble scheme and will be highly noticed by our Government. If Mr. Read is not promoted to a Captaincy no man in the Navy deserves it. If nothing turns up against us, this night will be an eventful one in the present war, and also in the history of every man connected with us.

Under a light breeze, Read and the *Archer* slid into Portland harbor and dropped anchor near Pomeroy's Rock, east of Fish Point, between Fort Gorges and the foot of Munjoy Hill. Read had easily entered the harbor, using coastal survey charts captured on his cruise along the Eastern seaboard. He and the other Confederates used their glasses in a careful survey of the fortifications as the *Archer* boldly slid past the trio of forts guarding the harbor's entrance.

The Confederate vessel dropped its anchor at 7:30 P.M. whereupon Read sent all but a few crew members below. Several men were left topside for appearances sake. The rest were put to work making oakum balls, soaked with turpentine, which were to be used to set fire to the *Agawam* and the *Poutoosac*.

At nine o'clock, Titcomb and Bibber, the two Falmouth fishermen who had been captured previously, were ordered below decks and tied up. They were told, "Men, don't attempt to come on deck tonight. Make no noise and resistance and it will be better for you." Bibber replied with a smart, "Aye, aye, sir."

Shortly afterward, the Confederate crew dressed in fishermen's clothes and stuck pistols and cutlasses in their belts. Read dressed in dark blue or black pants and a frock coat.

Lt. Read planned to begin his raid by seizing the steamer *Chesapeake* and gave every man verbal instructions. The crew was preparing to go topside when Eugene H. Brown, the engineer, told Read he did not think he could handle the *Chesapeake's* engine without the assistance of another engineer.

Read thought if he captured the *Chesapeake* Brown could do his duty and bring the engine up to steam. However, Read knew Portland nights were short in June and realized the Confederates would have a long wait while Brown readied the engine. Any long delay would make it impossible for the raiders to get clear of the harbor forts before they were discovered.

A moderate breeze was beginning to blow seaward, down the harbor. Read quickly decided to forget the Chesapeake and told his crew they would shift their attention to the *Caleb*

Cushing and seize it. Read also told the assembled men they would return to the inner harbor and burn other shipping after they had taken the *Caleb Cushing* past the harbor forts.

Two small boats were put over the side. Robert Mullins and two others were left aboard the *Archer* with orders to guard Titcomb and Bibber and to follow the rest of the crew to sea when they left in the *Caleb Cushing*.

The two boats full of raiders, one under Read's command and the other under the command of Master's Mate John E. Billups, headed for the *Caleb Cushing* at 12:30 A.M., after a dancing party had departed nearby Peak's Island and the harbor had returned to quiet.

Noting their approach, the *Caleb Cushing's* lookout hailed the Confederate's boats. However, the raiders simultaneously swarmed both the *Cushing's*quarters, before he could repeat the call. When they heard the oars

Donald Johnson
Fort Gorges on Hog Island Ledge guarded the entrance to Portland's inner harbor during the Civil War.

approaching, the cutter's watch had called to Lieutenant Davenport, who was sleeping in his cabin. The Lieutenant, bursting from his cabin in response to the call and the sound of feet on the deck, was quickly overpowered by four Confederates and ordered below, as was the deck watch.

The rest of the crew were turned out of their hammocks. The boarders had come equipped with handcuffs and in five minutes the entire on-board crew of the *Cushing* had been captured and secured. One of the crew had tried to escape through the fore hatch to swim ashore for help, but had been caught and sent below in handcuffs to join the others, already imprisoned in the forward part of the berthing deck.

Crew member William B. Kenniston, who had stood watch from 10 o'clock until midnight, had been in his hammock about a half an hour, and had just dropped off to sleep when he heard men climbing over the side and the sound of footsteps on deck.

"It's the new captain," he thought, "come to take command." The next instant he realized his mistake as a voice cried in his ear, "Surrender in the name of the Southern Confederacy!"

Read spoke to the cutter's crew once they had all been made prisoners. He told them, "Now boys, what we want is the *Cushing*, not you Yanks. If you behave yourselves, we'll put you off on some island as we go out of the harbor. If you make trouble you'll be shot and thrown overboard."

Lieutenant Davenport pleaded hard not to be handcuffed because he was a Southerner. His request was granted temporarily after he promised not to escape. However, he was soon put in irons like the rest of his crew.

Read went topside, leaving two Confederates with cocked pistols to guard the *Caleb Cushing's* crew. The rest of his men turned to and prepared to get the cutter underway. The topsail and topgallant sheets were out on the yardarms and had to be brought in and hooked to the clews. Running gear had to be cut adrift and the deck awnings had to be lowered and fastened out of the way.

The men were unable to slip the anchor chain and finally had to drag twenty-five fathoms of heavy chain aboard. The sail was hoisted and sheeted home. When Read attempted to get under way, it was discovered the *Caleb Cushing* was aground. A line was promptly run to a bark anchored ahead of the cutter and fastened to the vessel's mizzen chains. Hauling on the line, the Confederates soon hove their prize ahead to deeper water.

Problems continued to plague the raiders. The wind had fallen while they were preparing the cutter for sea, forcing Read to order twelve men into two small boats to tow the vessel out of the harbor. Starting against a flood tide, the raiders began to tow their prize toward the *Archer*, which was still anchored abeam of Fort Gorges.

At approximately 4 A.M. the *Forest City*, completing her run from Boston, steamed into the harbor and those awake aboard noticed the *Caleb Cushing* being towed out of the inner harbor.

Reuben Chandler, a *Forest City* crew member, interviewed years later said, "Coming in we passed the revenue cutter *Caleb Cushing* being towed to sea by two small cutter was a sailing craft. We did not stand close enough to recognize any of her crew, and there were only two men on the deck."

Abreast of Fort Preble a light breeze unexpectedly sprang up and the small boats were ordered alongside as the cutter accumulated speed.

Aboard the *Archer*, Titcomb and Bibber were brought topside and ordered into their rowboat, which had been brought alongside. They were quickly rowed to the *Caleb Cushing*, about an eighth of a mile away, and ordered aboard.

Read, rather than leave the harbor by way of the main ship channel, which would have taken him past the harbor forts, decided to leave via the Hussey Sound Passage, which lay on the far side of Peaks's and Hog Islands. Leaving Fort Gorges in his wake, Read asked Bibber, "Is there plenty of water?" The fisherman replied the cutter would be passing through shallow waters.

Implying Bibber was piloting the cutter, Read commanded, "Don't get this vessel aground!" Bibber remained topside and watched a crewman heave a lead to determine the water's actual depth.

One of the Confederate's prisoners was the cooks assistant, a boy of fifteen, who was released from his handcuffs and told to start a fire and prepare coffee. After the Confederates had

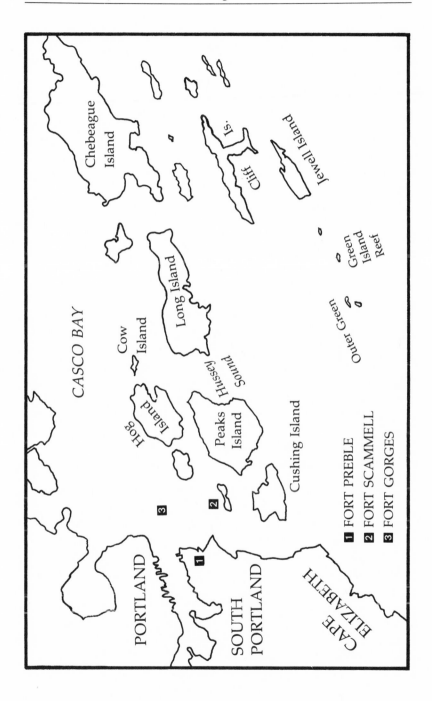

CASCO BAY

Chebeague Island

Is.

Clift

Jewell Island

Green Island Reef

Outer Green

Long Island

Cow Island

Hussey Sound

Hog Island

Peaks Island

Cushing Island

PORTLAND

SOUTH PORTLAND

CAPE ELIZABETH

1 FORT PREBLE
2 FORT SCAMMELL
3 FORT GORGES

eaten, the prisoners were given a breakfast of coffee and hardtack.

Read, shortly after talking to Bibber, had his first interview with Lieutenant Davenport, the cutter's former temporary commander, at breakfast.

Although a prisoner, Lieutenant Davenport had been treated with respect by his captors. Searching the ship, the Confederates had found Davenport's watch and chain. When the Lieutenant protested they were his, a Confederate gave them to him, saying they respected Davenport's "private property".

At breakfast Read told Davenport, "I'm sorry, Lieutenant, to meet you under these circumstances, but this is one of the fortunes of war. You, being a Southern man, ought to be ashamed of yourself."

Davenport retorted, "… you have acted humanly, sir, and in case we are taken I'll represent you favorably to the U.S. authorities."

Read again called upon Bibber for an opinion as the cutter came alongside the narrow passage between Cow and Hog Islands. Bibber was asked if the *Caleb Cushing* could go through the restricted passage. The Mainer replied it was a very bad passage. However, a breeze sprang up just as the cutter nosed into the passage. The vessel went through very quickly and was soon in Hussey Sound, heading for the open sea.

Reuben Chandler, of the *Forest City*, in his interview, described the excitement on the waterfront when the *Caleb Cushing's* disappearance had been discovered.

> When we reached the wharf, we encountered the Master-At-Arms of the Cushing, and naturally asked what he was doing ashore. When we told him we had seen the *Cushing* putting to sea, the cat jumped out of the bag. What a row there was then!

Jedediah Jewett, the port's customs collector, was having breakfast at 8 A.M. when he was notified the *Caleb Cushing* had been taken to sea. He immediately assumed that Lieutenant Davenport, a Southerner, had run off with the cutter.

Acting swiftly, Jewett, working with Portland Mayor Jacob McLellan, chartered four vessels to chase after the *Caleb Cushing*. In addition, he sent messages to two local Army commands requesting men and equipment. A message was sent across the harbor to Fort Preble requesting the assistance of the 17th Maine Infanty and to Fort Abraham Lincoln, up the Fore River at the end of the inner harbor, for manpower from the 7th Maine Volunteers.

Colonel E. C. Mason of the 7th Maine responded by having all the men in the camp, including the camp band, on the Portland waterfront within an hour.

Jewett chartered the *Chesapeake* and the *Forest City*. He sent the steam tug *Tiger* to the bridge in the upper harbor to transport the men of the 7th Maine Union Wharf, where they boarded *Chesapeake*. In addition, he chartered the *Casco*, a small steamer, to carry men and guns from Fort Preble to the *Forest City*, which drew too much water to dock at the fort.

The *Casco* transported 35 men, under the command of Captain Nathaniel Prime and 1st Lieutenant Edward Collins, and a 6-pound field piece and one rifled 12-pounder and a good supply of shot and shell across the harbor.

The *Chesapeake* was fitted out under the watchful eyes of Mayor McLellan and William F. Leighton, U.S. Naval Inspector, who assumed overall command of the vessel. Two brass 6-pounders, from the State arsenal, were put aboard the and placed under the command of G. T. Berry, a naval engineer, and a Lieutenant Waldron of the revenue service. A detachment of 27 men from Co.G, 7th Maine Volunteers, were placed aboard, armed and provided with ball cartridges. More than 50 citizen volunteers flocked over the rail.

One enthusiatic volunteer was James W. Brackett, a clerk with the firm of Fillebrown & Burton, which had its office at the head of Union Wharf. Writing in 1903, Brackett said:

> Great excitement prevailed throughout the city ... The neighboring merchants and clerks all visited the scene of the activities, each bringing back new and exciting reports ... I chafed considerably at my confignment at the store, especially as I had missed the Boston steamer's departure, and it now looked as though I would miss this also, as the proprietors of

the store in taking their turn at sightseeing had remained so long that I began to think my turn would come too late.

... I was seriously considering the propriety of bolting for the scene of excitement without notice, when the junior partner returned, saying to me that it was now my turn, and to be sure and not stay too long as business up to that time had been very much neglected. As he passed into the office I heard him say that when he left they were calling for volunteers.

This settled the matter for me ... I ran down the wharf, and, as I was passing, the Mayor held up a musket, shouting, "This is the last one, who takes it?" I was close beside him when he spoke, and reaching up took it from his hands and passed on to the steamer. For once I was in luck, for soon after boarding the steamer, orders were given for all who were not armed to go ashore. Mr.Oren Ring, father of Dr. Charles Ring, of this city, arriving too late to secure a musket, tried to buy mine, but I refused to sell, offering, however to loan him the bayonet, but at the last moment, a few of the volunteers suddenly remembered that they had important business elsewhere, thus enabling Mr. Ring to secure his passage ticket and remain on board.

A load of muskets were placed on board to be used by the volunteers, who were placed under the command of a Lieutenant Bachelder of the 7th Maine. Each volunteer was given ten rounds of ammunition. Ten kegs of powder were boarded, along with beef and hard bread to last the men for 48 hours. Bales of cotton, man-handled by the volunteers, were placed on the *Chesapeake's* rail and around her engines as protection from any shot fired by the escaping Confederates.

Arrangements were made with the Marine Observatory, located on top Munjoy Hill, to track the *Caleb Cushing* and, using signal flags, point out the course to the pursuers. The *Forest City* and the *Tiger* left the wharf first, followed by the *Chesapeake*, which took longer to get up steam.

CHAPTER TEN

THE DESTRUCTION OF THE CALEB CUSHING

The *Caleb Cushing* was approaching the tiny Green Islands, some five miles outside Portland Harbor, when fisherman Bibber asked Lt. Read to release him. Read refused. Two of the prisoners were brought from below, released from their restraints, and allowed to obtain water from the waterspout. Handcuffed again, they were returned below decks.

The tenacious Bibber, once the cutter was three miles beyond the Green Islands, asked again to be released. Read refused, saying he would stand off a little further out and wait for the *Archer* to join him.

The Confederates had been searching the *Caleb Cushing* for ammunition. They found plenty of powder, but no shot or shell. Questioned, the cutter's crew said they had received orders the previous day to search for the *Tacony* and had loaded power aboard, but had not loaded either shot or shell yet.

Actually, there were ninety-three rounds of thirty-two-pound shot and some shells in the concealed "apartment" adjacent to the captain's cabin, between the wardroom and his cabin. There was also shot in the wings on both sides of the powder magazine. Lieutenant Davenport had refused to show Read the shot locker's location, or to give the Confederate the keys to the powder magazine.

Nick Pryde, Read's gunner, found one thirty-two-pound shot in the ship's potato locker and carried it topside. The Confederates scoured the vessel, collecting pieces of scrap metal and ballast stones to use as ammunition. Read then ordered his crew, who had been up all night, to go below to get as much rest as possible.

Robert Hunt was assigned as helmsman and a small group of Confederates was detailed to guard the cutter's crew. Read ordered Hunt to keep a sharp eye out and also went below.

Hunt, about four bells in the forenoon watch, suddenly spotted a steamer coming out of the harbor. He called to Read, who hastened topside, and said he guessed it was the Boston boat, then returned below.

Subsequently, as the *Caleb Cushing* was passing Cod Ledge, Hunt again looked astern and spotted a second steamer leaving the harbor. Looking through his glasses he saw soldiers on the deck. He called to Read, who rushed to his side, took a hard look and called for all hands to clear the decks for action.

Prisoner Bibber scurried over to Read and begged to be released. Lt. Read replied he did not care what Bibber did and told him he could take one of the small boats that was tied alongside. Bibber clambered over the rail, tumbled into the nearest boat and began to row off, leaving his partner, Titcomb, still aboard the Confederate vessel.

Amidships, the thirty-two-pounder was loaded and Read gave the order to put the helm down as gunner Pryde and his crew trained the gun to get the steamer's range. But, the cutter would not mind her helm.

"Hard down!," shouted Read as he jumped toward the helm.

"Hard down it is," helmsman Hunt replied.

"Oh for a six knot breeze and a few shot and shell," cried Read, "We would show them some fun."

The two steamers were directly in the *Caleb Cushing's* wake and when Read saw his crew would have trouble gaining a good shot he shouted, "We will give them a scare anyway!".

The gun was trained as far aft as possible and Pryde pulled the lanyard. When the smoke cleared, both steamers were seen to be broadside, as if turning back. The Confederates gave a loud yell and cried, "Load her up again...!"

The Marine Observatory, back Portland's Munjoy Hill, reported to Mayor McClellan the *Caleb Cushing* was about 12 miles from Cushing Island, which lies at the entrance to the main ship channel, and was bearing south-south-east from Portland Head Light. The lookout could see the *Forest City* in the van, with the *Tiger* close behind. The *Chesapeake*, the last of the pursuers to leave the wharf, was bringing up the rear.

Aboard the *Forest City*, the officers assembled and debated what action they should take as the steamer neared the cutter. The consensus was that the *Forest City* should continue after the *Caleb Cushing* and hail her as to her intentions. However, the discussion had barely finished when those aboard the *Forest City* witnessed a flash from the now broadside cutter and the sound of her gun came booming across the water. At this point only two or three miles separated the vessels.

Second, third, fourth and fifth shots quickly followed. The last of the missiles came within thirty feet of the *Forest City*, which stopped dead in the water. Then, observing the *Chesapeake* drawing close with a bone in her teeth, the *Forest City* hauled off out of range and bore away to meet the rapidly approaching New York-line steamer.

One reason the *Forest City* pulled back was to protect her exposed paddle wheels. The last shot from the Confederates made it obvious that the side-wheeled steamer could easily be disabled and left helpless in the water by a well placed shot.

Also, there was a great deal of confusion among the officers and volunteers aboard the steamer. Captain Nathaniel Prime, 17th U.S. Infantry, wrote in his after action report:

> When we were [within] about two miles, she opened fire upon us ... none hitting us. I regret to say I was not in the position to take the stand my inclination dictated; the steamer was filled with citizens without any knowledge of the responsibilites of the situation, and who apparently had left the harbor for a pleasure trip. The accumulated advice and disjointed comments of these bewildered the captain, who stopped his boat and awaited the arrival of the propeller Chesapeake ...

Maine Historical Society

The steamer *Forest City.*

A shot from the cutter, intended for the *Chesapeake*, ricocheted across the water. It was followed by another. The order was given to try the *Chesapeake's* port gun as an experiment. It was a good line shot, but failed to touch the cutter.

The Portland newspapers, reporting the day's events later, claimed the Confederates had run out of shot and had been forced to load their guns with pieces of iron, ballast stones and even a round Dutch cheese. *Chesapeake* volunteer James W. Brackett, later said: " But, certainly the howling over our heads indicated something more indigestible than cheese ... matters began to look more interesting, and it began to look as if the affair was going to be something more than a picnic."

The *Chesapeake* came alongside the *Forest City* and slackened speed. Both vessels were within the *Caleb Cushing's* range and a well-directed shot would have been a calamity to the pursuers. However, out of ammunition, the Confederates had ceased fire.

"Ship ahoy!," shouted Captain Leighton and the *Forest City* answered back, "What course do you intend to take?"

"Can't you attack from one side, while we attack the other?", asked Captain Leighton aboard the *Chesapeake*

"We think the best course is to run her down, as she has the superior armament, " replied Captain Liscomb of the *Forest City*.

"Will you take the lead?", shouted Leighton.

Liscomb declined, saying, "No, you had better go ahead, we are not prepared."

"All right," said Captain Leighton, "we shall steer straight for her and run into her any way we can, and you can take what's left!"

Captain Leighton, Colonel Mason and several others had been watching the *Caleb Cushing* from the apex of the *Chesapeake's* pilot house. Leighton, after hollering back and forth with Captain Liscomb of the *Forest City*, looked down at the eager volunteers on the deck below and told them it was a question of the *Chesapeake* sinking the *Caleb Cushing* or the *Caleb Cushing* sinking their steamer. He called on all hands to vote on what action the *Chesapeake* should take next.

Maine Historical Society
Captain John Liscomb of the *Forest City*.

It was unanimously voted to run the revenue cutter down by striking her amidships. If this failed the *Cushing* was to be boarded by the enthusiastic volunteers. Everyone loaded their weapons as the *Chesapeake* bore down on the Confederate vessel at fifteen knots.

Colonel Mason turned to his men and said, "Now boys, you have got to fight, let every man keep cool and await orders, and we will take the cutter." Those on the *Chesapeake* gave three cheers, which was answered from the *Forest City*. Someone on the *Chesapeake* shouted "Stand by your flag!" to the *Forest City's* crew.

Someone else shouted an order to be ready to board the cutter.

James W. Brackett, in his account of the action, wrote: "Not being much of a sailor, I remember looking over the side of the steamer wondering how, with that ungainly musket in my hands, I was to get from the high deck of the steamer to the lower deck of the cutter without either breaking my neck or falling overboard."

The Confederates aboard the cutter, discovered they had fired every possible missile they had been able to find. Read knew their cutlasses and pistols would not dissuade the men aboard the swiftly approaching steamers. Immediately, he gave the order to set fire to the *Caleb Cushing* and to abandon the vessel.

The prisoners were brought from below, told they were being set free and assisted over the starboard rail into two small boats. Someone on the cutter threw a handful of keys into one of the boats when the prisoners protested because they were still in handcuffs. However, the prisoners slipped their oars into the water and pulled away from their Confederate captors without even stopping to unlock their restraints.

Robert Hunt and a shipmate aboard the cutter jumped into the Captain's cabin and proceeded to splinter the furniture and tear up the bedding to make a fire. The second man found a can of camphene and sprinkled it over the mass of bedding and demolished furniture. Hunt struck a match to ignited the camphene's fumes. Instantly, the flames jumped to the sodden mass of bedding, which burst into a column of fire.

Hunt and his companion, fearing for their lives, bolted up the companionway. Gasping for air on the main deck, Hunt discovered his eye brows and moustache had been badly singed and that both of his hands had been severely blistered by the turbulent flames.

Read, gathering his crew together, produced a handful of money, which he dealt out. The Confederates then climbed over the rail and dropped into the remaining small boats, which had been tied on the port side. However, before abandoning their prize, the raiders unbuckled their belts and removed their small arms, which they dropped into the water.

The Southerners pulled away from the blazing *Caleb Cushing* and fastened a white cloth to a boathook as a crude flag of surrender.

Aboard the *Forest City* , Captain Benjamin Willard, who had been acting as a harbor pilot, proposed the volunteers get into small boats and board the *Caleb Cushing*, rather than tear up the cutter with shot and shell. A number of volunteers piled into boats and began to pull away from the *Forest City*, when someone noticed the Confederates pouring over the cutter's side.

"They've fired her," yelled Captain Willard, "and there's a ton of powder aboard! She'll blow sky high when the fire hits that!"

Aboard the nearby *Chesapeake*, which had slowed considerably, two men contended for leadership of the volunteers. One of the would-be commanders was Nathaniel Harris, who owned a hat shop on Portland's Middle Street. The other was Charles Knapp, the port's Shipping Master.

The small boats carrying the cutter's original crew, still in handcuffs, were rapidly pulling toward the *Chesapeake*. The cutter's men feared those aboard the pursuing steamers would think them Confederates. Only Lieutenant Davenport was wearing a white shirt, which was quickly ripped off his back and fastened to an oar and raised on high. However, aboard the *Chesapeake*, the excited volunteers failed to notice the sign of surrender dangling from the oar.

As soon as the *Caleb Cushing's* boat came within gun range of the steamer, Captain Knapp, aboard the *Chesapeake* jumped

The steamer Chesapeake

Mariner's Museum, Newport News

on top of a cotton bale and ordered, "Fire, boys! Fire! They are going to board us."

The men in the boat, hearing Knapp's frantic order, dropped their oars and held their handcuffed hands over their heads and cried, "Don't shoot! Don't shoot!"

The volunteers vacillated and Colonel Mason of the 7th Maine, sword in hand, sprang onto a cotton bale and threatened, "The first man who fires I will run him through." From this moment it was clear to the volunteers the Colonel had taken command.

Almost immediately, Captain Leighton, who was still atop the pilot house, noticed one of the men in the small boat was waving a small handerchief. He yelled, "Hold! The first man that fires shall be shot; I am not a pirate to fire on a flag of truce!"

The handcuffed men in the small boat were helped over the *Chesapeake*'s side and escorted below, still in their restraints. As he struggled aboard, a noticeably disturbed Lieutenant Davenport protested to his rescuers, "It is hard, after a man has been taken prisoner, ironed and his life threatened by pirates, to be shot by his own friends!"

Samuel Prince, one of Davenport's crew, years later expressed similiar emotions when he said:

> We had been through a hard, trying time, and [all] we had expected to get from the men on the steamer was sympathy and condolence. In this we were bitterly disappointed. To be surprised and captured by a gang of men from we knew not where; to be manacled, and carried to sea; to be under the fire of the steamer pursuing; all this was hard and not without danger, but to be hissed and hooted at and called traitors and every defrauding epithet in the language by those from whom we had looked for friendliness and kindness was harder yet and we could not understand it.

The reason the *Caleb Cushing's* crew was sent below, still in their irons, was simple. Many on board, not knowing the facts, thought the *Caleb Cushing* had been taken by Lieutenant Davenport, whom they knew to be a Southerner. They assumed Davenport had bribed the crew and had been taking the *Caleb Cushing* to a Southern port.

The *Forest City* had picked up Read and his men while the *Chesapeake* was retrieving Davenport and his crew. The Confederates' reception was no better than that given to the cutter's crew.

Later, Robert Hunter described how he and his shipmates had been brought aboard the *Forest City*, "One man at a time was allowed over the side. He was searched and then his arms tied behind his back with a piece of rattling stuff and placed under guard before another was taken on board."

The *Caleb Cushing* continued to burn in the background while the captains of the two steamers held a shouted consultation . They decided to wait and watch the cutter blow up before setting a course back to Portland.

Several bold souls aboard the *Chesapeake* begged Captain Leighton, "Give us a small boat, Captain, and some buckets and we will board and save her." Leighton, more level-headed, replied, "You must not go ... she has four hundred pounds of powder on board, and the experiment is hazardous ... foolhardy!"

However, several of the more tenacious among the volunteers convinced Henry Fox, the *Chesapeake's* agent, to lower a small boat. As soon as it was lowered, six men climbed down into it.

The *Chesapeake* put on steam and ran to within a half-mile of the *Caleb Cushing*, then turned and headed back toward Portland. The men in the small boat, which was still tied to the steamer, called for volunteers and buckets, but received neither. After going about three miles the propeller-driven *Chesapeake* turned back towards the *Caleb Cushing*, which had been burning for approximately an hour.

Finally the *Chesapeake* took up position about a half-mile from the flaming cutter, while the *Forest City* laid to a quarter mile away. The tiny tug *Tiger* stopped about another quarter mile behind the *Forest City*

The *Caleb Cushing* was afire both fore and aft. Several schooners and fishing boats were lying to some distance from the action and assorted small boats were rowing about, but none dared approach the burning vessel.

The six men in the *Chesapeake's* boat saw a small boat secured to the cutter's stern and decided to save it. Three of them climbed back aboard the *Chesapeake* and the other three cast off the line and pulled for the *Caleb Cushing*.

After rowing a quarter of a mile, they heard orders being called to them from the *Chesapeake's* deck to return to the steamer. They replied, "You need not order us, for we shall not come until we bring the cutter's boat."

The three were soon alongside the cutter, which was blazing from stem to stern. The flames had mounted the masts and were beginning to race across the sails.

One man jumped into the cutter's small boat, which was two-thirds full of water, only to find he did not have a knife to cut her free. Fingers flying, all three men struggled to untie their prize while they were bombarded by falling cinders and pieces of flaming rigging.

At last the cutter's boat was free and the three had their sodden prize halfway back to the *Chesapeake* when there was an horrendous explosion.

Smoke rolled up in vast columns as fragments of shells, masts, spars and blackened timbers were blown hundreds of feet into the air. The cutter began to sink immediately, her stern slipping downward into the boiling water. The *Caleb Cushing* careened, lurched and slid out of sight.

James W. Brackett remembered the explosion this way:

> It was a grand sight. For a moment a red glare enveloped the hull of the vessel, pushing a heavy cloud of smoke and flame high in the air. Through this could be seen pencils of bright light shooting through the whole mass, carrying with them the upper part of the vessel broken into innumerable fragments, the whole mass pausing a moment in mid- air, then dropping with a crash into the water ... and the *Caleb Cushing* is no more.

Fisherman Bibber, in the small boat Read had given him, was picked up by the *Forest City*, which turned and started toward Portland. As she left the scene of the *Caleb Cushing's* destruction, several crewmen spotted a suspicious-looking schooner near Jewell Island. Bibber informed everyone it was the *Archer*, which had been captured the day before by Read and used to tow the *Caleb Cushing* out of the harbor.

The *Forest City* pursued the fleeing schooner and fired a shot, which passed between the *Archer's* wheel and her after cabin. Robert Mullins of New Orleans, who had been left in command of the schooner by Read, swiftly decided it would be best to put the helm down and heave to. The *Forest City* drew alongside and found three Confederates and Bibber's partner, Elbridge Titcomb, aboard the last Confederate vessel to cruise Casco Bay.

The *Chesapeake* ran alongside to provide assistance, but not being needed, turned and headed for Portland, to be followed shortly by the *Forest City*, which was towing the *Archer*. Behind them a group of small boats and fishing craft were already picking up wreckage from the *Caleb Cushing's* explosion.

The vessels arrived in Portland about four P.M. The harbor forts fired their guns as the tiny flotilla steamed up the ship channel. Church bells were rung and the wharves and shore were lined by eager citizens, who acclaimed the steamer's passage.

Read and his men were put ashore on a Portland wharf, where soldiers with fixed bayonets strained to hold back an outraged mob. The Confederates were quickly moved across the harbor to Fort Preble, where they were marched up the hill to the fort under a substantial guard.

The road to the fort was lined by an enthusiastic crowd of men, women and children. Many citizens welcomed the prisoners with jeers and cries of "How does your neck feel, Johnny Reb?" and "Hang the pirates!"

The Confederates all breathed a sigh of deliverance when they reached Preble's sallyport, where they were met by Colonel George T. Andrews, who told the crowd, "Shame on you, citizens of Portland. You do not know how to treat a captured foe."

Back in Portland, the tired volunteers from the *Chesapeake* were marched to Barnum's Restaurant on Temple Street, where a dinner was served, probably in lieu of paying the men prize money.

The still angry mob constantly ragged at the *Caleb Cushing's* crew as they were marched to the Portland jail. They were held overnight and then released after a brief investigation into what was rapidly becoming known as the *Caleb Cushing* Affair.

Maine Historical Society

A sketch of the destruction of the *Caleb Cushing* by Portland artist Harrison B. Brown. Compare this sketch with the cover illustration.

Nine of the cutter's crew asked for and received immediate discharges from the United States Revenue Service. They said they did not wish to serve on another ship with three or four of their shipmates, whom they claimed had shown the "white feather" when the *Caleb Cushing* had been taken by Lt. Read.

The cutter's crew did not complain about their overnight confinement, but did complain about the suspicions and abuse to which they had been subjected the previous day.

The Portland *Eastern Argus*, praising the *Caleb Cushing's* crew said:

> Let the people of Portland and the State give the credit due these men, not for their action, for they had no chance to act, but for their loyalty and patriotism in refusing to tell where the ammunition was, which, had they not done, would have cost us many precious lives, and brought about, mayhap, many different results. Let due justice also be done Lieut. Davenport, who, although a Southern man, is a favorite with these loyal men, and should be with all loyal citizens.

A large number of artifacts from the *Caleb Cushing* affair where displayed at various Portland locations.

The *Archer's* captors had discovered a large stash of goods and materials aboard the schooner, which Read and his men had plundered from other ships. This booty included six chronometers; a variety of sailing direction books and coastal pilot books; three barrels of beef; 32 pairs of lambs wool sox; 28 bags of seaman's clothing; seven muskets; a brass 12-pound howitzer; five cartridge boxes; a double-barrelled fowling piece; three American flags; a French flag; and seven cotton toilet covers.

One man was killed when a musket was accidently discharged while being unloaded from the *Archer*.

Three flags captured aboard the *Archer* were hung between the pillars in a large room at the Custom House. The oakum fireballs, which had been soaked with turpentine by Read's men, were exhibited at the Merchant's Exchange on Middle Street.

The *Caleb Cushing's* small boat, which had been rescued from the stern of the flaming cutter, was renamed the *Trio* and placed in the boathouse of the North Star Boat Club.

The *Tacony's* log, which had been maintained after her capture by Read, was sent to Secretary of the Navy Welles in Washington.*

Read's carpet bag, which his captors set aside for safe keeping when he surrendered and which was put aboard the *Forest City*, had disappeared. It contained the bonds of captured vessels, a small amount of gold, the papers of vessels the Confederates had destroyed, and Read's instructions from Captain Mafitt of the *Florida*. The bag turned up a day later when the *Forest City* returned from her regular Boston run.

Harrison B. Brown, an artist of growing Portland fame, and one of the volunteers who had chased the *Caleb Cushing*, created a sketch of the moment the revenue cutter was destroyed by the explosion. Photographic copies were made and sold at Larrabee's store on Exchange Street.

---

*Early in July 1863, the half-burned hulk of the *Tacony* was towed into Cape Cove, Nova Scotia.

CHAPTER ELEVEN

ESCAPE FROM FORT WARREN

Charles W. Read and his men had been confined at Fort Preble for only a few hours when an angry delegation from Portland arrived insisting they be given custody of the Confederates.

Led by City Marshal Heald, the force, which consisted principally of policemen, demanded to take charge of the Confederates and transport them to Portland's jail. George L. Andrews, the fort's commander, bluntly informed the locals that the Confederates were prisoners of war, properly under his care, and were being held under a strong guard.

Heald and his men stormed back to Portland, where the marshal scurried to inform Mayor McLellan his forces were prepared, if their assistance was required, to prevent the prisoners' escape from the fort.

The excitement quieted down late in the evening, only to be rekindled after midnight by the clamor of alarm bells. At approximately 3 A.M. a dispatch carrier arrived at Marshal Heald's office to report a Confederate privateer was standing offshore, landing men on Cape Elizabeth.

Elizabeth Gould, then a young girl living with her family on Pearl Street, was awakened by the bells' din. Dashing from window to window, she expected to see the sky radiant from a nearby burning building. The sky, however, was still dark. Peering across the street she could just make out white-clad figures in the windows of the house opposite. Recognizing a friend, she called, "Where's the fire?" Neither the friend nor anyone else knew, and still the bells kept ringing.

Finally, Jim Lowell, a friend passing by in the street, reported, "There isn't any fire, but the rebels are this side of Portland Light!"

Years later Elizabeth Gould described how her family responded to this fearful information:

> Oh, oh, oh! May I never again have such a sinking of heart! In a few minutes every member of the family was up and dressed. The Major (then a Lieutenant and home for a few weeks) got out his pistols and cartridges. A younger brother who had been down the harbor ... and who went to the front a few months later, was provided with a belt and weapons and both were off in a few minutes. Father started for the bank to "move the coin," if the report proved true, for this was a time of paper dollars and fractional currency or shin plasters and coin was coin.
>
> We women planned and talked in solemn quiet. Should we stay or go? If we staid should we prepare for death? If we went, where and how and what should we take with us? Mother wanted to take a few treasured relics in her hand and start on foot for Gorham or Freeport — dear mother who found Congress Street a distance that taxed all her strength. She thought she would "cut father's oil portrait out of its frame and take it along, and the baby's picture!" We girls with the hopefulness of youth refused to believe that all was lost just yet

Across the harbor in South Portland, a long drum roll sounded across the parade ground at Fort Preble and sleepy troops turned out, prepared to repel an unknown number of Confederate raiders. On the Portland waterfront a noisy crowd of citizen volunteers clambered aboard the *Montreal*, ready to rush to the scene of the invasion. However, they calmed down and went ashore after the alarm bells stopped ringing.

The whole incident had been akin to the acorn falling on Chicken Little's head. A tug had been seen close to the Cape Elizabeth shore and someone assumed it was a Confederate vessel.

A week later the hysteria over another Confederate raid on Portland assumed comic opera proportions. On July 7th a small coastal survey steamer entered the port, passing between Forts Preble and Scammell. The ship entered the harbor at full speed and neglected to signal her intentions to either bastion.

A Lieutenant Inman, at Fort Preble, clearly seeing his duty, ordered a blank cartridge fired across the steamer's bow. The vessel did not respond to Inman's warning and continued into the harbor.

Inman then commanded his gun crew to fire a shot across the steamer's bow, which caused the craft to instantly reverse her engines. However, the shot was a ricochet, which skipped across the main ship channel and plowed ashore at Fort Scammell, demolishing an outhouse. Several soldiers who had been clustered around the doomed structure quickly scattered, escaping injury. Later the Lieutenant boarded the survey steamer and explained his action.

Several days later the United States Revenue Cutter *Dobbin* arrived in Portland to replace the destroyed *Caleb Cushing*. The vessel took up a guard position at the entrance to the inner harbor opposite Fort Gorges, which at night was normally manned by only a small group of volunteers.

On the afternoon following their surrender, Read and his officers were visited by William F. Leighton, who had commanded the *Chesapeake*, and a man named Hallett of Hyannis, Massachusetts, a passenger on the *Tacony*, when Read captured her earlier.

During the visit, Hallett discovered one of Read's men had his watch, which was hastily returned to him. After he returned to Portland, Hallett found half of his belongings, lost during the *Tacony's* capture, among the *Archer's* booty at the Custom House.

While talking to Read's officers, Captain Leighton recognized Lieutenant Brown, Read's engineer. Leighton remembered Brown had served on the frigate *St. Lawrence* during the Paraguay expedition of 1859, when Leighton was aboard the a sloop-of-war *Preble*, which took part in the same expedition.

Several members of the local press, including a representative of the Associated Press, also visited Read and his crew at Fort Preble, where the Confederates were being confined, unshackled, in two large rooms separated by a well-guarded corridor.

A Mr. Berry of the Associated Press, speaking for the press group, declared they would like to ask the Confederates a few questions, but were not there to "pump" them, insisting they would be satisfied with whatever information they procured.

Read, who had been reading a book when the reporters arrived, quietly outlined the Confederates' cruise along the Eastern seaboard. One of the press later described Read as a " ... spare, diminutive man, decidedly inoffensive and reserved in his manner, and the very last person one would suppose willing to embark on the hazardous expedition in which he has been the leading spirit."

The same reporter characterized Lieutenant Brown as having a face "constantly wreathed in smiles, particularly when mention was made was made of their [the Confederates'] burning vessels, ... he seemed to gloat over."

The *Evening Courier's* reporter wrote a narrative which described the rest of Read's officers:

> The remaining officers were Master's Mates. Their names were as follows: — N. B. Pryde, who belongs in New Orleans, La.; John Billaps, Mathass County, Va., and James Mathewson of New Orleans, La., all of whom are native of the South, but the last one and he is a Scotchman. Mr. Billaps is tall and well proportioned, with quite a high forehead. A merry twinkle constantly played about his eyes. He had but a few words to say, but seemed to enjoy heartily all allusions to their exploits. Mr. Pryde is a tall slim man, while Mathewson is thick set, very dark complexioned with a keen penetrating black eye. He was the only one among the officers that a person would have singled out as a desperado.

All of the officers told the reporters they were confident they would soon be exchanged for Union men imprisoned in the South.

Portland July 12th 1863

Dear George.

Better late than never so I will
sit down and and write you a letter.
I received your letter all right a good
while ago. I have been sick but am all right
now. I suppose you have heard how the
rebels came into the harbor and stole
the U. S. Revenue Cutter Caleb Cushing
but in the end got a little of the worst
of it. *sent to capture the "Rebels"* There was fun here when the vessels
got back to see the people who went in
them, some of them had guns without
bayonets, and some had flint locks and
with any thing they could get. Ministers
were making cartridges, store keepers clerks
seamen &c were on board and all for a fight
The next night there was an alarm that the

Frank P. Wood
**A letter from Charles H. Chase of Portland in which he describes
the Confederate raid on Portland Harbor.**

The journalists then stepped across the double-guarded corridor and visited Read's seamen, whom they decribed as a "villanous set of men." According to the visitors the men were stretched out on the floor singing "Way down in Alabama" and other Southern songs and "wore a sullen look when gazed at."

Read's crew told the trio the Confederate government allowed them twenty-five percent of all the property they captured, which was apportioned among the crew in twentieths, according to rank.

Although they were prisoners of war, both Read and Brown were allowed to send to a nearby store for sardines and soda biscuits to make snacks. Later they acquired cloth samples from a Portland tailor, who made them new clothes. All the purchases were paid for with gold, of which Read seemed to have plenty.

Read was allowed to send mail and composed a letter to Alphonse Barbot, another Confederate, who was imprisoned at Fort Lafayette, New York. Read, apparently had access to newspapers, for he wrote:

> My Dear Barbot:
> As I have just noticed your arrival at Fort Lafayette, in company with the officers and crew of the late ram Atlanta, I have concluded to drop you a few lines, informing you of my being bagged, and nicely closeted, in a well-built fort in "Old Abe's" dominions.
> ... It was my intention, when I came into Portland, to cut out a sea-going steamer, but, strange to say, at the decisive moment, Mr. Brown (whom you will remember in connection with the breakdown of the *Arkansas* engine) declared himself to be incompetent to work the engines of the steamer, unless he had another engineer to cooperate with him. All my plans were then crushed, and I was compelled to take the cutter out as a *dernier resort...*
> We have been kindly treated by our captors. I expect we will be sent either to New York or Boston in a few days. As they have commenced exchanging again, I hope we all may be sent into Dixie before long. My kindest regards to Trav and Williamson. Write to me.

Williamson was Midshipman John A. G. Williamson of the *Atlanta*, also a prisoner at Fort Lafayette. The *Atlanta*, an ironclad ram, had been captured at Wassaw Sound, Georgia on June 17, 1863 by the monitors *Weehawken* and *Nahant*. Her crew was transported to New York and confined at Fort Lafayette, just off the Brooklyn shore.

Read and his crew were not exchanged as he had hoped. However, he and his men joined Barbot and his crewmates when both Confederate groups were tranferred to Fort Warren in the middle of Boston Harbor.

Fort Warren, located on George's Island, commanded the access to Boston Harbor and was often imputed to be the "Gibraltar of the North." During the war more than 1,000 Confederates were confined at the fort.

The construction of Fort Warren commenced in 1825 when work began on the seawall along the east and northeast shores of the island. Work on the fort itself began in 1834. The fort's outer parapet rises to a height of 69 feet above sea level and encloses a 12 acre area. Its inner walls are constructed of eight-foot thick segments of granite and are from 600 to 666 feet long.

James Homer, a writer for the *Boston Post* who visited the fort in 1845, marveled:

> You ascend a long flight of stone steps. Having touched the ground you walk about forty feet, and then turn to the left, when you find yourself in the 'prison-house' of the fort, which extends, through several apartments or sections, a distance of over one hundred feet, and is capable of accommodating one thousand prisoners, if we should ever have as many in New England, which is at least problematical ...

Fort Warren was commanded by Colonel Justin T. Dimick, who had graduated from West Point in 1819. Dimick, a career soldier, had fought Indians in Florida, had served on the Canadian border and had been a field officer in the Mexican War. The fortress was garrisoned by Massachusetts troops who treated the Confederates with respect.

The colorful Boston Cadets were stationed at the fort during the summer of 1862, and throughout the rest of the war the First Massachusetts Heavy Artillery Battalion served at

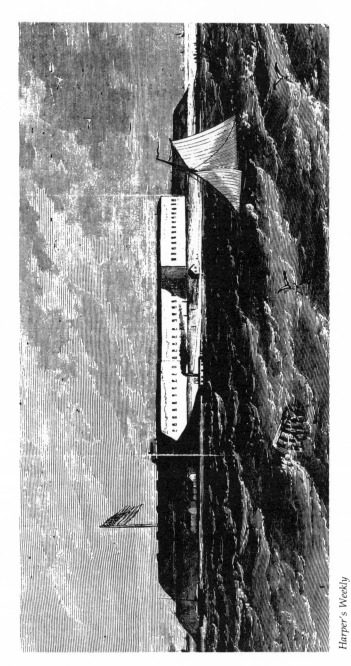

Fort Warren in Boston Harbor.

Harper's Weekly

George's Island. Late in 1861, the 1st United States Artillery Regiment band was sent to Fort Warren, where they stayed for the duration of the war.

In the Fall of 1861, officials in Washington decided to send a hundred political prisoners, many from the border state of Maryland, to Fort Warren. Meanwhile, since the Army planned to move the political prisoners, who were being held at Fort Lafayette, New York to Fort Warren on the steamer *State of Maine*, the commander of nearby Fort Columbus, located on Governor's Island, decided to send another 600 Confederate soldiers to the Massachusetts fort.

On October 31, 1861 a surprised Colonel Dimick greeted the arriving prisoners by saying he had only expected a hundred men and had only prepared quarters for that number. Compounding the problem, food supplies ran short almost immediately.

The Boston press published sympathetic accounts of the situation and the city's citizens responded by donating food, beds and other supplies. In addition, the rules in force at that time allowed the wealthier political prisoners and officers to obtain food from Boston caterers. Lawrence Sangston, a Maryland legislator, later boasted: "Our mess continues to improve; fare now equal to any of the hotels; the only trouble is I eat too much for so little exercise." At the same time enlisted prisoners from North Carolina, no matter what the weather, had to prepare their meals outdoors in large pots.

Life at Fort Warren, especially in the beginning, was not difficult for the Southerners. The prisoners were even allowed pets. Lieutenant Joseph W. Alexander of the *Atlanta* had a small English terrier, Fanny, with him at the fort. The little dog earned the affections of a Union commissary sergeant who used to bring a daily ration of fresh beef to Fanny. However, the Confederates took the meat and gave the dog the bones.

Eventually, however, the authorities in Washington, who had learned of the liberal treatment of the Confederates, took away the men's special privileges. They were no longer allowed to send to Boston for special food supplies and could only eat the uninviting prison food.

Miller's Photographic History
Confederate prisoners at Fort Warren. Number 21 is Charles W. Read and number 24 is Joseph W. Alexander.

The richer Baltimore politicians, and the officers from North Carolina, who had been captured at the fall of Fort Hatteras, occupied quarters originally intended for the garrison's officers, while enlisted men and civilan prisoners lived in casement rooms.

Read and his men and the *Atlanta's* crew, were housed in the casements under the main battery. During the day they were allowed to exercise on the pavement in front of their quarters, but were locked up at sunset. Throughout the night, armed sentries paced back and forth outside their doors.

Escape from Fort Warren was thought to be impossible. The men were enclosed in a granite fortress, strictly guarded night and day, and confined behind solid walls constructed to withstand the battering of heavy gunfire.

Four of the Confederates, Lieutenant Joseph W. Alexander of the *Atlanta*; James Thurston, a Lieutenant of the Confederate Marine Corps stationed on the *Atlanta*; Reid Sanders, a political prisoner from Kentucky; and Charles W.

Read, the Portland Harbor raider, resolved to escape. The four constantly discussed the possibilities and rejected many plans.

In the cellar beneath the room where the men were confined was a pump which provided their water for bathing. The eight-foot walls of this basement room were perforated by two musket loop holes, approximately six feet high and three feet wide on the inside, which gradually narrowed to a width of seven or eight inches on the exterior.

Lieutenant Alexander, washing up one day in the pump room, was struck by the idea he could crawl through the musketry hole. Boosting himself up, he managed to get his head through the narrow opening by turning as if he were looking over his shoulder. However, his clothing prevented his body from passing through the opening.

Quickly, stripping naked, he tried again. With difficulty he found he could squeeze through the eight-inch gap. Elated, he hastily dressed and dashed upstairs to tell his three companions of his discovery. Sanders, Read and Thurston, all of whom were smaller than Alexander, each found they could easily pass through the hole. At once, the quartet made plans to escape.

On the next dark night, the four descended to the pump room, slipped through the loop hole and lowered themselves into the dry moat between the main batteries and those facing the water. Cautiously, they crawled over the unmanned water battery and wriggled through the grass, slowly making their way toward the sea wall at the water's edge. There, their worst fears were confirmed when they discovered guards had been posted on the wall. The sentinels were pacing back and forth; when they met they would turn and walk away from each other.

The escapees waited and, one by one, passed over the wall as the guards departed. Their heads pressed against the cold granite and their feet submerged in the chilly water, the men huddled at base of the wall and nervously deliberated their next move.

A stiffening wind had begun to pound surf against the sea wall where they stood. Offshore, a chop was beginning to roughen the channel between themselves and neighboring Lovell's Island, their immediate objective.

The four concluded it would be too dangerous under this condition to attempt to swim across the channel. Frustrated, but undefeated, the Confederates, climbed back over the sea wall, dodged the sentries, and made their way back to the musketry loop hole. The escapees had planned ahead for such a setback and had asked other prisoners to hang a rope from the loop hole, which they used to pull themselves back into their prison.

Only a few of the other prisoners knew that the four had been outside of the prison. Many even ridiculed the idea that anyone could get through such a small space as the musketry loop hole. One midshipman, noticing the quartet's wet clothing, actually tasted the cloth and was convinced when he savored the ocean's salt.

The prisoners were not disheartened by their initial failure to escape from the Gibraltar of the North. Read suggested that two of his men, Nick Pryde, formerly the *Tacony's* gunner, and Thomas Sherman, both qualified swimmers, join the next attempt. Read spoke to them and both agreed.

The Confederates' new plan called for Pryde and Sherman to swim to Lovell's Island and steal a boat. The duo would then sail or row their prize close to the George's Island shore, whereupon Alexander, Thurston, Sanders and Read would swim out to meet them.

The next evening, July 19, 1863, the six escapees made their attempt. The original four lowered themselves into the ditch, where they were joined by the two new recruits.

Read, Alexander, Thurston and Sanders concealed themselves in the grass between the water battery and the wall. Pryde and Sherman crawled on, passed between the patrolling sentries and made their way into the water.

They were never seen again!

The remaining quartet huddled in the grass and waited for what seemed like hours, until they quietly decided to make a move on their own. Since Reed and Sanders were poor swimmers, all agreed Alexander and Thurston would swim to Lovell's, obtain a boat and return for the others.

One of them noticed a small target, made of light white pine and used during the day by the guards for firing practice, which they hauled along the shore to where they planned to enter the water.

Alexander and Thurston planned to drape their clothes over the target and thrust it ahead of them as a float while they swam to Lovell's Island.

As soon as the guards had begun walking towards the opposite ends of their posts, the Confederates vaulted the wall and hauled the target into the water. However, before they could get away from the island the guards returned and stopped to talk just above their heads. Worse still, Read and Sanders, who had plunged into the water to assist Alexander and Thurston, were still clinging to the barely floating target.

The guards continued their idle dialogue until the prisoners heard one say, "Where's the target? Wasn't it here when we came on post?"

"Yes," replied the other. "Where can it be," he wondered aloud as both men walked to the edge of the wall, and stared into the dark shadows beneath their feet.

In the blackness the four escapees lay close together, barely daring to breath.

Suddenly one sentry exclaimed, "I believe I see something down here in the water." "Stick your bayonet into it and see what it is," urged the other.

The guard lowered his muzzle and shoved it toward Read, who was immediately below him. The bayonet's tip actually came to a stop on Read's chest. Read held his breath and never moved a muscle.

The threat only lasted a moment, whereupon the sentry protested, "I am not going to stick my bayonet into saltwater." The two discussed the target's disappearance for a few more minutes and finally concluded "spirits had taken it away."

They separated and resumed marching their posts. Alexander and Thurston tied their clothes to the target and pushed off to Lovell's Island. Read and Sanders climbed back over the wall and hid in the grass.

Weakened by a lack of exercise while in confinement, the swimmers were also numbed by the cold water, even though it was July. In addition, the tide was pulling them away from Lovell's Island.

Bug (or Narrows) Light lay opposite the end of George's Island and the two attempted to keep the flashing beacon to their right as they pushed ahead through the darkness.

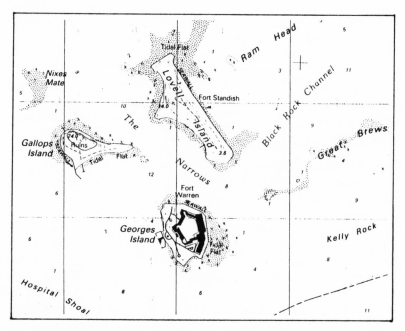

Fort Warren and environs in Boston's outer harbor.

After what seemed like hours, the nearly exhausted Confederates stopped for a minute, allowing their feet to sink under them. They were surprised to find they could touch the bottom. Mustering their diminishing strength, they waded ashore, towing the target after them.

Almost frozen, they started to search the small island for a boat. Fearing to separate, they kept together, eventually finding their haven to be uninhabinated.

In time they discovered a small schooner-rigged fishing boat, which had been pulled up on the beach and anchored. They dragged the anchor up to the bow and tried to nudge the craft into the water. The vessel was small and should have immediately slid away from the shore, but for some reason it stayed in place.

Again and again, a frustrated Alexander and Thurston pushed and pulled the boat back and forth at the water's edge. Then they discovered a second anchor line secured to the stern.

Quickly cutting the line, they tugged the boat into the water, raised the sail and set a course for George's Island. The sky had been brightening for some time, but it was not yet daylight. The pair planned to drop the canvas and row close to the shore as they neared Fort Warren.

It was broad daylight when the men hove to off George's Island. They could clearly see the sentries pacing along the wall and did not dare to edge closer to shore for fear of arousing guard's suspicion. They also could see that Read and Sanders had left their positions near the wall.

Alexander and Thurston sailed past Fort Warren and headed out of Boston Harbor into Massachusetts Bay. When they were well away from land they set a course for St. John, New Brunswick, the closest neutral Canadian port.

Read and Sanders had waited for Alexander and Thurston until almost daylight and were detected while attempting to return to their casement. They were placed in close confinement and the alarm was sounded.

Officers from the fort immediately sent two sailing vessels after Alexander and Thurston and called for a fast steamer to join the chase.

Pushed by a light breeze, the fleeing Confederates sailed northward along the Massachusetts coast until afternoon, when they ran close to shore to locate food and water. The duo were only wearing hats and shirts, having lost their pants during the swim to Lovell's Island.

A mile east of Rockport, Massachusetts, the Confederates beached their boat to talk to a group of boys playing on the sand. The escapees asked the boys for food, saying they had not eaten for twenty-four hours. Several of the lads ran into town, where they told about the strange men at the beach. The alarmed townspeople immediately headed for the shore, but when they arrived the fugitives had put to sea again, steering in the direction of Portsmouth, New Hampshire.

About dusk, the Confederates nosed their schooner in close to Rye Beach, New Hampshire, where they saw a man standing in front of a house. They hailed him and requested he come to their assistance, which he did in a small boat.

Suspicious, the stranger listened as the Confederates spun a tale of having "sailed out from Portsmouth on a lark." They said they had been swimming and their clothes had blown overboard while they were in the water. They asked for clothing and something to eat and drink.

The man rowed ashore and returned with some old clothes, a bit of food, some tobacco and a bottle of plain brandy. Alexander felt the man knew who they were, although he said nothing when the Confederates thanked him and told him they were going to anchor just off the beach for the night.

As soon as their benefactor left and was out of sight, the pair set a course for Eastport, Maine, intending to land in nearby New Brunswick. However, the wind soon dropped and they lay becalmed most of the night. Alexander took the helm until midnight, when Thurston relieved him.

Neither men had slept for two nights and Alexander immediately fell asleep. He awoke in broad daylight to find the boat off course in a light breeze.

Because the wind did not pick up until forenoon, several other sailing vessels lay in sight most of the morning. Around nine o'clock, Alexander noticed a large schooner scurrying from ship to ship. The men immediately realized the schooner, which later proved to be the United States Revenue Cutter *J. C. Dobbin*, was searching for them.

The *Dobbin* hailed and questioned a large number of vessels until she queried the schooner *J. Baker*, Captain Barbrick, of Boston, who reported they had just passed a schooner-rigged yacht which was acting "very strangely." The schooner in question was lying to the windward and the *Dobbin* made straight for her.

Around noon, between Boon Island, Maine and the Isles of Shoals, New Hampshire, the *Dobbin* came alongside and hailed the Confederates' small boat. Alexander and Thurston said they were Eastport fishermen who had been to Boston for some fun and were now headed back home. The cutter's crew was about to let them go when someone suggested the two "fishermen" be searched. The cat was soon out of the bag! One of the men was found to have a water-soaked gold watch and a large amount of Confederate money secured around his waist.

Both captives were ordered aboard the *Dobbin* and their small boat was tied to the cutter's stern. The *Dobbin* then set a course for Portland. A short time later the steamer *New Brunswick*, enroute from Boston to Portland, glided alongside the slower *Dobbin*.

Captain Webster, aboard the cutter, grabbed his speaking trumpet and shouted to the *New Brunswick*: "How many prisoners escaped from Fort Warren?" The answer came back, "Three."

"We've got two of them on board, " replied Webster.

Further conversation was useless as the faster *New Brunswick* quickly pulled away from the cutter. The steamer reached Portland early in the evening and brought with it word the Fort Warren escapees had been re-captured.

Captain Webster treated Alexander and Thurston kindly and told them the *Dobbin* and other vessels had been searching for them for two days. When the cutter arrived in Portland the Confederates were handed over to the United States Marshal, who immediately handcuffed Alexander's left wrist to Thurston's right wrist, which made Alexander "feel very queer."

Years later, speaking of his handcuffed arrival in Portland, Alexander said:

> We must have presented a sorry spectacle on landing, for a little newsboy seemed to feel very badly about us. He ran off somewhere and came back with two apples, which he gave us. A crowd was collecting about us, and the marshal put us in a cab and carried us to the city jail and delivered us to the jailer, who took us upstairs and put us into cells adjoining each other.

The Confederates could talk back and forth, but could not see each other. Alexander later said: "The food furnished us in this jail was certainly the most disgusting ever offered to men."

Several days later the prisoners received a bundle of clothing from their comrades in Fort Warren. With their clothes came a message saying Read and Sanders were well, but were being kept in close confinement.

Alexander and Thurston were kept in separate cells at night, but were allowed to be out for a short time during the morning and then were locked up together in one cell. Their imprisonment caused great excitement in provincial Portland.

The jail was crowded with visitors who came to see the "rebel pirates", as the prisoners were called by the locals. Alexander later remembered:

> They would come and stand at the doors of our cells and discuss us as if we were a species of wild animals; and I suppose we were a kind of menagerie to them. After a while we got used to being stared at and paid no attention to them. ...
>
> Several of the visitors were evidently very sorry for us, and some few books were sent us by some kind people of the city; but, as a general thing, the people were very bitter, and told us plainly that they thought we ought to be killed.

Alexander and Thurston were kept in the Portland jail for about a month. During that time they plotted an escape.

They were confined in cells on the second floor. The bars on the cell doors were about an inch thick. The Confederates planned to saw through the bars and make their way to the first floor washroom, where they would remove one or two of the bars and climb through the opening. They were determined to reach Canada, either by stealing a boat or by making their way across country.

It took them a while to obtain a tool to saw through the bars, but eventually the slow work began. However, the men were transferred back to Fort Warren before they could make much progress.

Once in Boston, they were kept in close confinement for several months. Colonel Justin T. Dimick, the fort's commander, offered to put them with other prisoners if Alexander and Thurston promised not to attempt to escape. His offer was refused and Alexander and Thurston had begun plotting to escape from their room when they were suddenly put back with the other Confederate naval officers in their original casement.

Undaunted Alexander at once started looking around to see how escape from the casement might be possible. There were two stack chimneys in the room, which meant there were two flues in each chimney, one for the fireplace in Alexander's casement and one for the fireplace in the adjoining one.

Alexander, together with Read and others from the *Tacony* and the *Atlanta*, decided to remove the partition or divider in one of the chimneys and climb out the top. They doggedly began the work, fully realizing the task would take many months.

The fireplaces had been closed up and only a hole for a stovepipe remained. The officers took down enough bricks to let one man into the fireplace, where he began enlarging the flue by removing the partition bricks one at a time. Those taken out of the chimney were beaten into dust and taken out in the slop buckets every morning.

Taking turns, the men worked all night. The facing bricks were replaced at dawn each morning. Bread was used to replace the mortar and the bricks had to be whitewashed before the weary Confederates climbed back into their beds for an hour's sleep.

The work went on for months and the partition had almost been removed when the men discovered a sentry posted at the top of the chimney. Their wearisome labor had all been in vain.

Eventually the naval officers, Alexander and Read included, were exchanged at City Point, Virginia, for Union officers who had been captured by the Confederates.

CHAPTER TWELVE

JOHN CLIBBON BRAIN

SWINDLER AND SPY

Most of his life John Clibbon Brain was an engaging confidence man, swindler and bunko artist. During the Civil War, however, Brain rose to the heights of glory by hijacking three vessels for the Confederate cause.

The first of these prizes was the steamer *Chesapeake*, already famous along the New England coast for the part it played in the capture of Charles W. Read and the Confederates who seized the *Caleb Cushing* in June of 1863.

The *New York Sun* called Brain one of the most "picturesque adventurers of the Confederacy". Little has been written about this adventurer, whose Civil War exploits filled columns of newsprint in both the United States and Canada.

John Clibbon Brain was born at Ball's Pond, Islington, London on May 30, 1840. In London, John Brain, John Clibbon's father, an unsuccessful copper plate dealer and engraver, had led a bohemian life and had been forced to declare bankruptcy in 1845.   The family emigrated to the United States in May 1849 aboard the packet *Ivanhoe* of the Black Star Line and settled in Springfield, Ohio. However, young John's parents soon separated. His mother remained in Ohio while his father moved to Montgomery, Alabama. Later, he re-located to Holly Springs, Missouri.

U.S. Navy.

John Clibbon Brain.

John Clibbon Brain inherited a measure of his father's artistic ability and gained a basic knowledge of the printing and engraving trade early in life. Brain always insisted his name was spelled Brain, not Braine as reported by the contemporary press.

Little is known about his development as a young man except his disregard for the work ethic.

Shortly before the Civil War, Brain married a girl from the Williamsburg section of Brooklyn, New York. The marriage lasted many years. The honeymoon, however, was a clear indication of Brain's approach to life. The *New York Times* later commented:

> ... His first venture, so far as is known, was in Williamsburgh, Long Island, were he became acquainted with a young woman of poor but respectable connections, whom he eventually made his wife. After marriage, they went on what is technically called a "honeymoon", touring through the West, stopping at leading hotels by the way, and stepping out to the tune of the "free list." Arriving at an extreme point West, the "Lieut." finding that he was "played out" on that line, left his wife as security for a hotel bill. The landlord in this case declined the agreement, and the young wife returned to Williamsburg ... At length the "Lieutenant" dropped her a note, and she left. This was about the time when the rebellion broke out. A few months only elapsed before Mrs. B. returned to Williamsburgh, loaded down with luxurious apparel, so much so as to astonish her old friends with the splendor of the transformation. Her purse was lined with gold and she was unaccountably rich.

In an 1892 application for a pension from the State of Tennessee John Clibbon Brain claimed, "I was commissoned a Master in the C. S. Navy at Montgomery, Ala in May 1861 immediately after my resignation from the US Navy. I was afterwards promoted to First Lieutenant and First Lieutenant Commanding ..."

During the war the Northern press frequently referred to Brain as "Lieutenant Braine." There is no official record indicating John Clibbon Brain ever held the rank of Lieutenant in any navy. The United States Navy records in the National Archives do not contain any material proving Brain ever served with the United States Navy. However, those records do indicate Brain was appointed a Master, not in the line of promotion, in the Confederate States Navy on May 26, 1864. In addition, *The Register of the Commissioned And Warrant Officers of the Navy of the Confederate States*, published in Richmond in 1864, under the heading of "present duty or station", lists John C. Branie (sic) as being on "Special duty".

Arrested in Baltimore in 1903 for obtaining board and lodging at a hotel under false pretenses, Brain told the police he had joined the Confederate Navy as a midshipman and had risen to the position of Commander. He boasted to a reporter from the *Baltimore Sun* he had received a commission as a Master and later was promoted to Captain.

However, Brain neglected to tell either the Baltimore police or the press he had been arrested in Michigan City, Indiana in September of 1861, charged with being a spy for the Confederacy, and with being both a member of the secret Knights of the Golden Circle * and an officer in the rebel army. He was committed to jail in La Porte, Indiana for want of $ 6,000 bail and had to wait for a grand jury to meet. Subsequently, by the order of Secretary of State William H. Seward, he was transferred to Fort Lafayette, New York for safekeeping. Later, he was transferred to Fort Warren in Boston Harbor.

Apparently Brain possessed a camera when he was captured. The *Chicago Journal* reported: "John C. Brain, a daguerrotypist, was arrested at La Porte, Ind., as a member of the K. G. C. and a Southern spy."

It is not clear from the available records whether Brain was actually functioning as a spy, or engaging in a swindle, or both. One of his usual con games was to tell a railroad company or a hotel that he was producing a railway guide, and then request free transportation or lodging. In addition, Brain would raise funds by selling subscriptions for the promised guide.

---

* Formed in Cincinnati in the late 1850's by George Bickley as a filibustering organization to create an empire for the K.G.C. in Mexico. Rumors in 1861 claimed that K.G.C. members were seeking to get Kentucky to secede and join the Confederacy. It was during this period that Brain was supposed to be a K.G.C. member.

John B. Thomas, a Chicago attorney, reading of Brain's arrest in the *Chicago Journal*, wrote a scathing letter to the Sheriff of La Porte County:

Chicago, September 7, 1861

Dear Sir:

If the John C. Brain spoken of in the above extract taken from the *Chicago Journal* of this date is more than medium size, light complexion, light hair and greyish eyes, with rather exposed upper teeth when speaking, and if the said John C. Brain has at any time been engaged in getting up a railway route book from New Orleans to New York, the said John C. Brain is an unmitigated scoundrel and swindler, and if the evidence is not sufficient to properly punish him on the charge of spy to the enemies of our Government hold him for swindling several parties of this city and of Pittsburg of considerable sums of money and advise me by mail. I think William D. Baker, Shanley S. Milar, S.P. Rounds, proprietor of the Adams House, of this city, or a Mr. Haven, a publisher and printer of Pittsburg, Pa., would be glad to get a chance at him.

When arrested, Brain was carrying a paper indicating he was one of eight men authorized to form several fledgling companies for the Confederate Kentucky State Guard. It listed John C. Brain as being a Sergeant. Another document authorized Brain to enlist men for the companies to be called for when needed. Some of the papers were written in a cipher.

Brain and his wife, who was not arrested, had been living temporarily at the Jewell House in Michigan City, Indiana. Michigan City was the junction of two railroads, the Louisville, New Albany & Salem and the Michigan Central. Brain's papers included a letter from J. B. Anderson, Superintendent of the Louisville & Nashville Railroad, asking station agents to assist Brain in making sketches along the railroad's route.

Federal officers, reporting to Washington, hinted that Brain might be an agent for the shipping of contraband goods to Louisville, Kentucky. Mary Farley of La Porte swore Brain had tried to arrange with her to carry revolvers to Kentucky and Tennessee. The La Porte woman claimed Brain had promised that both he and his wife would accompany her on the covert journey and that she could earn $30 a month smuggling contraband to the South.

Brain showed Mary Farley a handbill calling for men to enlist in the Southern army. Later, Mrs. Brain destroyed the handbill, together with some of Brain's other papers, by throwing them in a sewer.

The swindler-spy-smuggler had been arrested after having been suspected and watched for some time. Brain had raised the suspicions of the Superintendent of Louisville, New Albany & Salem Railroad. The contraband agent had obtained a pass on the railroad in order to gather information for a traveler's guide or map of the line. It was probably a typical Brain scam, because the superintendent later observed that John Clibbon Brain never seemed to be gathering any information, for he frequently disappeared for as many as seven to ten days.

Several persons related to Federal officials how Brain had told them he was a member of the Knights of the Golden Circle and had urged them to join that secret society. E. M. Davis testified Brain had discussed forms of government with him and reported Brain preferred one like France's.

Brain fabricated different stories about his background. He told one Federal official that he was a citizen of New York State, and told another that he was a native of Tennessee and that he had a brother in the Confederate Army. He also told the latter officer he had been given a Confederate commission, but preferred to "seek his fortune" in the North by creating railway guides.

He also claimed to have been the editor of the *Southern Traveler* of Baltimore.

Brain, an accomplished swindler, later charged Federal officers had stolen $200 in gold from him at the time they took him into custody. The officers reported Brain was penniless and owed his hotel bill when he was arrested. In fact, Brain owed a Mr. Lower of Michigan City sixteen dollars for a coat he purchased. Learning that Brain had been arrested, Lower journeyed to La Porte and demanded Brain either pay his bill or return the coat. Brain insisted he was broke and said he would pay when he was ready. At that point, Captain William

Copp, Company B, Ninth Indiana Volunteers, whipped the coat off Brain's back and gave it to Lower. Copp later called Brain an "impudent scoundrel".

Arrested by the military, Brain had been turned over to the civilian authorities in La Porte. Secretary of State Seward ordered John Clibbon Brain sent to Fort Lafayette in New York harbor as a suspected disloyal person. Fort Lafayette already housed a large number of "disloyal" citizens from Baltimore and elsewhere, as well as several crews from captured blockade runners and privateers.

Brain was first sent to Fort Hancock on the Brooklyn shore and then transferred to Lafayette, a quarter of a mile out in the harbor. He was met by Lieutenant Charles O. Wood, the fort's commander, then shown to his quarters in a first floor casement.

Fort Lafayette prisoners who had money were charged $1.00 a day for their meals, which were better than those provided by many second class hotels in 1861. Brain, who was broke, ate the pork, beef, potatoes and coffee given to the post's common soldiers twice a day.

Two hours of each day, one at dawn and one at dusk, were devoted to exercising the prisoners on the parade ground. The prisoners were locked in their casements at dark and all lights were extinguished at nine o'clock.

The prisoners amused themselves during the day by visiting from casement to casement, reading the New York papers, smoking cigars and by playing whist and backgammon. No gambling was allowed.

John Clibbon Brain, imprisoned almost within sight of his Brooklyn home, used his time to begin a campaign to secure his release. On October 4, 1861 he wrote E. M. Archibald, the British consul in New York:

> I have been removed from La Porte, Ind. after being confined over a month in the county jail to this fort. When arrested or till now there has been no distinct charge against me and I am guiltless of any unlawful act. The soldiers who arrested me took from me over $200, giving no receipt or acknowledgement whatever. By the Chicago newspapers I learn that I am an officer in the rebel army, the only foundation for which has

been my having signed the roll of a company of State Guards in Kentucky which company I believe has never been organized and I never took any oath whatever to this country or State thereof. I am a native of London; came here in 1849; have never been naturalized or declared intentions ... As a British subject I appeal to you for protection and the restoration of my money and liberty.

Secretary of State William H. Seward, contacted by the British embassy in Washington, allowed Archibald to interview Brain at Fort Lafayette. However, on October 26th, Seward wrote Lord Richard Bickerton Pemell Lyons, the British minister to Washington:

> ... [Brain] is imprisoned as a person dangerous to be at large during the existing condition of affairs in that State and in others. He is detained at a place where the writ of habeas corpus is suspended and it is conceived cannot at present be released compatibly with the public safety.

Lord Lyons and Secretary Seward exchanged a series of letters regarding the Brain case over the next few months. Seward's position was that Brain had engaged in "treasonable practices", while Lord Lyons questioned whether or not the public safety required that Brain be detained further. During this period Brain was transferred from Fort Lafayette to Fort Warren in Boston harbor.

In what was later proved to be a gross misstatement, Lord Lyons wrote Seward on January 11, 1862 saying, "The letters he [Brain] has written to me and to her Majesty's consuls are those of a man of so little education that I do not think he can be very dangerous." Seward replied immediately to question Brain's assertion of British citizenship.

Brain himself wrote Lord Lyons to say his five month imprisonment was telling fearfully on his health. He offered to swear he would not go to any of the Southern states or do anything hostile to the United States, saving his allegiance to the Crown of Great Britain.

Snatching the bait, and ridding itself of a naggingdiplomatic problem, the State Department instructed Colonel Justin Dimick, Fort Warren's commander, to free John Clibbon Brain after Brain had signed an oath agreeing to the terms he proposed in his letter to Lord Lyons.

Colonel Dimick, February 10,1862, witnessed Brain's oath:

Fort Warren, Boston Harbor, February 10, 1862

I, John C. Brain, a prisoner confined in Fort Warren do solemnly swear that I will neither enter any of the States in insurrection against the authority of the United States Government nor hold any correspondence whatever with persons residing in those States without permission of the Secretary of State; and also that I will not do anything hostile to the United States during the present insurrection. So help me God.

John C. Brain

In signing this letter, John Clibbon Brain, had executed his biggest scam!

Just out of prison and broke, Brain disappeared from the public eye as soon as he reached the Boston waterfront. According to the *Quebec Mercury* he journeyed to Montreal, where his married sister lived.

The *Mercury* reported Brain had obtained an introduction to officials of the Grand Trunk Railway, which ran between Montreal and Portland, Maine, and had announced he was going to publish a *Grand Trunk Railway Guide*. He also said John Lovell, prominent Montreal printer, would print his publication.

Lovell was dismayed to learn Brain had been collecting large amounts of money for advertisements and subscriptions to the proposed guide book. Brain had never paid Lovell a satisfactory deposit and when challenged he refused. Lovell told Brain to stop using his name in his solicitations.

The *Mercury* also reported Brain had never paid the engravers he retained to do work for his guide. Brain disappeared from Montreal owing several hundred dollars.

The elusive swindler tried his luck in Quebec and then left for England, where he enjoyed some success with the same scam in Liverpool and Manchester. He spent a few days visiting relatives in Nailsworth, Gloucestershire, before returning to North America.

A State Department copy of John Clibbon Brain's oath.

He appeared in Halifax, Nova Scotia in the summer of 1863 and presented himself as "J. C. Brain, publisher, Montreal, C. E." According to a Halifax newspaper " ... he took the tone of a plodding, peddling sort of body, who was anxious to turn an honest penny by publishing a book ... "

Calling on Halifax's business community, the erstwhile publisher said he was preparing to issue *Brain's Mercantile Statistical Work, and Business Directory of Canada and the Provinces.* As usual he solicited advertisements and subscriptions for his announced publication and obtained various sums, ranging from twenty-five shillings to twenty-five dollars in advance.

Papering his scram, Brain gave his marks receipts, which he completed and signed:

> Published under the patronage of the Grand Trunk Railway Of Canada. John C. Brain, publisher, Montreal, C. E.
>
> Received from .... £ 1 5 s., for which I agree to insert in Brain's Mercantile and Statistical Work, and Business Directory of Canada and the Provinces, to occupy space of one fifth page. I also agree to deliver, free of charge, one copy of said work.
>
> £ 1 5s.
>
> Jno. C. Brain

Elsewhere on the receipt Brain signed a promise to deliver his book in eight months. As he had done in other communities, Brain also disappeared from Halifax, leaving behind him a string of unpaid bills and a large number of angry subscribers and advertisers.

John Clibbon Brain, formerly a "plodding, peddling" man, re-appeared in Halifax six months later in the guise of a swashbuckling Confederate raider, a hunted man, who had stirred up a hornets nest along the New England, New Brunswick and Nova Scotia coasts by hijacking the steamer *Chesapeake* on its run from New York to Portland in December of 1863.

Swindler or Confederate, John Clibbon Brain was to disprove Lord Lyons claim that he was not a "very dangerous" man. The man who pledged to "not do anything hostile to the United States" was to be the last Confederate prisoner of war held by the United States.

CHAPTER THIRTEEN

HIJACKING THE CHESAPEAKE

Leaving a number of swindled advertisers and unpaid bills behind him, John Clibbon Brain travelled to New York and New Jersey in the fall of 1863. While in the latter state he met Vernon Locke, a native of Nova Scotia who had been living in South Carolina for twenty years. Locke frequently used an alias, calling himself John Parker.

Originally from the Ragged Islands, a small chain of islands near Shelburne, Nova Scotia, Locke at one time owned several coastal vessels trading with the West Indies. It was rumored he had engaged in smuggling on more than one occasion.

On October 27, 1862, Confederate Secretary of State Judah P. Benjamin issued a letter of marque to Captain Thomas B. Power of the *Retribution*, who in turn transferred it, with his name to Vernon Locke, alias John Parker. The letter of marque allowed private citizens like Power to equip a ship with arms and attack Union shipping. However, the right granted by the letter was vested in the ship and not in the captain.

Locke, a British citizen who had taken an oath of allegiance to the Confederacy, probably used an alias to avoid the serious penalties involved in breaking the British neutrality laws.

The *Retribution* started her life as the *Uncle Ben*, a Lake Erie tugboat. In April 1861 the U.S. Navy requisitioned the tug as part of a unit being sent to support Fort Sumter. Enroute, a violent storm forced the vessel to seek shelter in Wilmington, North Carolina, where local citizens seized her, converted her to a gunboat and turned her over to the Confederacy. Late in 1862 the former tugboat's engine was transferred to the *C.S.S. North Carolina* and her hull was sold to a group of new owners who re-fitted her as the *Retribution*.

During her short career as a privateer, the *Retribution* captured three vessels, the brig *J.P. Ellicote* , the schooner *Hanover* and the brig *Emily Fisher*. However, the former lake boat become unseaworthy and was sold in Nassau, the Bahamas.

Locke, whether he knew it or not, lost any status as a commander of a Confederate privateer when the *Retribution* was sold.

The die was cast once Vernon Locke, the one-time smuggler and privateer, and John Clibbon Brain, the former spy and swindler, met by chance in Jersey City after Brain disappeared from Halifax in the fall of 1863.

The two wanted to hijack a Union vessel and either take it south to the Confederacy or use it themselves as a privateer. They decided on the latter action and travelled to St. John, New Brunswick in mid-November to a obtain a crew and to complete their plans to seize a Northern steamer.

Brain and Locke were soon holding a series of meetings in a Main Street workshop in the Cove section of Carlton, a St. John suburb. Most of those attending were British subjects and residents of St. John and the surrounding area. The St. John *Evening Globe* later said: "They are the worst species of humanity, denominated "Roughs", one of them just being out of the penitentiary."

The first recruiting session was sparsely attended, but twenty men showed up for the second. Brain and Locke conducted the gatherings, assisted by Henry A. Parr, a Canadian, who had been living in Tennessee the past seven years.

During the second meeting, Brain announced he wanted twenty men to go to New York and capture a steamer on behalf of the Confederacy. Locke produced a paper which displayed a large official looking seal signed by Jefferson Davis. He said it was his commission from the Confederate government, although it was more likely the *Retribution's* letter of marque. Both men claimed to be Confederate officers and Brain told the men he held the rank of lieutenant.

The men were told their passage to New York would be paid by Parr and that they would share in the proceeds of seizing the steamer, but it was unclear as to whether they

The recruiting meeting in the Cove section of Carleton.

were also to share in the proceeds of both the ultimate sale the steamer and its cargo. Some crewmen later recalled being told they would receive $500 if the captured steamer were successfully taken to Wilmington, North Carolina. Others remembered the discussion centering around taking the vessel to Nova Scotia.

No target steamer was mentioned by name. However, Brain and Locke must have had the Chesapeake in mind because Brain and Parr had sailed from New York to Portland early in November to check out the steamer and its her crew. Brain had even taken his wife and one of his children along to provide him with a "cover".

The men were told that once they were in New York they were to go, individually, to a certain store and pick up a package containing a revolver, ammunition and a pair of handcuffs.

Ultimately, fourteen men decided to join Locke, Brain and Parr in the effort to hijack a steamer.

One of the men was thirty-year-old David Collins of Loch Lomond, a small farming community on the outskirts of St. John. Collins had a pleasant countenance, but was somewhat stooped and practically bald. His father was a hard-working farmer and a Methodist preacher. One of his brothers was the Reverend John Collins of Maine; and another was Captain William Collins of the 15th Mississippi, who in June of 1864 was to lead the Confederate raid on Calais, Maine.

On December 2, 1863, Vernon Locke, alias Captain John Parker, gave John Clibbon Brain his marching orders:

To Lieut. Commanding, J. Clibbon Brain

You are hereby ordered to proceed to the City of New York and State of said, with the following: 1st Lieut. H. A. Parr; 2nd Lieut. David Collins; Sailing Master, Geo. Robinson, and a crew of 11 men. You will on arrival there engage passage on board the steamer and use your own discretion as to the proper time and place of capture. Your action towards crew and passengers will be strictly in accordance with the President's instructions. You will as circumstances permit, bring your prize to the Island of Grand Manan for further orders, Seal Cove Harbor, if accessible.

John Parker
Capt., C. S. Privateer *Retribution*

Locke, a civilian with no legal authority to act for the Confederate government, proceeded to grant David Collins, the minister's son, a Confederate commission:

To David Collins:

Reposing confidence in your zeal and ability, I do hereby authorize and commission you to hold and assume the rank of 2nd Lieutenant and this shall be your authority for any act, under order from me, against the Government of the United States, or against citizens of the United States, or against the property of either, by sea, or by land, during the continuance of hostilities now existing. This commission to bear the date from the 1st day of December, A.D. 1863.

John Parker

The authority to grant Confederate commissions rested with Jefferson Davis and the government in Richmond. Vernon Locke, a British subject, did not have the authority to grant a commission to David Collins, another British subject.

On Thursday, December 3, 1863, Brain and his men sailed for New York aboard the *New England*. Several of the men who had attended the recruiting sessions but declined to enlist in the questionable enterprise, went to the dock to see the others depart.

Surprisingly, little notice was taken of the large number of able-bodied men among the passengers aboard by the *New England* by its officers and crew or by officials in Eastport, Portland or Boston, where the steamer stopped.

The editor of the *Colonial Presbyterian*, who was a passenger on the short St. John - Eastport run, later told a St. John newspaper:

> There were not as many passengers as usual, and but few ladies, but the number of young men was remarked and remarkable. We noticed that one of them, not unknown to us, passed by a name other than his own, in getting his ticket. We ... learned enough to convince us that an organization for a daring attempt on the Federal commerce was in progress, its headquarters being in New York, and its ramifications in Canada, Nova Scotia and New Brunswick. ... There seemed to be about fifteen of the party, 'Colonel' Braine, so called, being their leader. They were bound for New York, and left the impression on our mind that they designed an attack on one of the steamers of that port. They were undoubtably armed, and might readily have captured the *New England*.

Previously, on at least three occasions, Boston's police chief had placed special police aboard the vessels running between Boston and St. John to frustrate rumored Confederate plans to seize a steamer.

Arriving in New York, Brain and his men crossed the Hudson River and checked into a hotel in Jersey City, New Jersey, and registered as having arrived from "Nassau, Bahamas". Their heavy baggage failed to attract any special attention and the group kept to themselves.

The *Chesapeake*, a 160-ton passenger and cargo steamer which had played a major part in the chase after Charles Read in the *Caleb Cushing* Affair, was scheduled to depart from Pier No. 9 at three-thirty Saturday afternoon, December 5, 1863 on her regular run to Portland, Maine.

On Saturday morning, eight men purchased tickets for the voyage at the Cromwell Line's ticket office on West Street. The men boarded the steamer, refusing offers of help and carrying their own baggage aboard.

Brain, the consummate con man, represented himself as an agent for an English steamship company and was given a free pass.

The rest of the hijackers arrived at the dock as the *Chesapeake* was pulling out into the East River and had to be rowed out to the vessel. Once aboard, they pretended not to know any of the other passengers.

The *Chesapeake* sailed from New York with sixty tons of coal aboard to fuel her boiler, only enough fuel for three days and not enough for a round trip. Her sail was rather small and according to Captain Isaac Willett was "not to be depended on without auxiliary power". The *Chesapeake* was manned by a crew of eighteen and carried twenty-two passengers, including Brain and his thirteen men.

The *Chesapeake's* only armament were two six-pounders mounted on the bow and a handful of revolvers in the possession of Captain Willett and several crew members. The vessel and its cargo were valued at $160,000. The cargo itself was typical of that carried by any coastal steamer and included such ordinary items as three crates of crockery, twenty-one barrels of flour, eleven boxes of stove polish, and forty-five boxes of tin. Four cases of wine were aboard for H. H. Hay, a prominent Portland drugstore, while 100 casks of wine were bound to Quebec merchants. Ninety bales of cotton and 108 boxes of starch were being sent to the Bates Mill in Lewiston, Maine, while 131 bales of rags were slated for a paper mill in Gardiner on the Kennebec River.

The *Chesapeake's* cruise along the Long Island shore went routinely and the vessel was soon leaving Nantucket and the hook of Cape Cod behind to port.

On Sunday evening, Captain Williams of the schooner *Betsy* plucked a bottle containing a letter from Long Island Sound. Unsigned, the letter raised more questions than it answered:

ON BOARD *PATAPSCO*

Sunday morning daylight

Last night, about 12 o'clock, the Captain and officers of the *Patapsco* were seized by a gang of ruffians, between 20 and 30 in number, who had taken passage on board in New York. They were all well armed and among their number were engineers and sailing masters, who immediately took charge of the vessel. The passengers had nearly all retired, and all hands were so completely surprised that resistance was out of the question. The Captain and officers were handcuffed and confined below, as were also the passengers. I throw this overboard in a bottle ..

TWO HOURS LATER - There has been a great bustle on deck. A vessel is alongside and cannon is being transferred to our vessel. The craft alongside is a steamer, and from what I can see of her she is pierced for cannon. From conversations overheard I gather that there were two other vessels near by to co-operate with them. Look out for a formidable raid somewhere.

Captain Williams landed in New York with the letter, giving rise to a series of rumors about the hijacking of a mystery steamer, since there was no vessel named the *Patapsco* in New York waters. The authorities never determined who had thrown the bottle into the Sound. It is not known whether Brain and one of his men had set it adrift in the hope it would confuse the authorities after the *Chesapeake's* seizure was discovered.

By midnight Sunday, December 7th, the *Chesapeake*, her decks coated with ice, was fourteen miles north-northwest of Highland Light, Cape Cod. From here the course would be straight across Massachusetts Bay to the Cape Elizabeth Lights, twin towers marking the outer entrance to Portland Harbor.

First Mate Charles Johnson was in charge, assisted by a two-man deck watch. Second Engineer Orin Schaffer supervised the engine room, where fireman Patrick Connor was fueling the boiler.

A drawing of the Chesapeake.

Dennis Mallet

At 1:30 in the morning on December 8, 1863, Johnson left the pilot house to get a cup of coffee in the cabin. He had just begun to drink his coffee when he heard a pistol being fired in the nearby engine room. Dropping his full cup to the deck, he threw open the engine room door and looked down into the engine area, where he saw a man pointing a pistol up at him. The man fired, but the shot missed and struck the massive piston cylinder.

The shot Johnson heard had been fired at fireman Connor by the hijackers. The ball missed, but came close enough to burn his face. Second Engineer Orin Schaffer clambered up into the fire room from the lower engine room just as Connor was being placed in handcuffs.

When he realized what was happening to his fireman he roared, "Stop fooling with the men!" George Wade, one of Brain's men who had been shackling the firemen, wheeled and fired his revolver directly into the second engineer's face. Schaffer buried his face in his hands but tried to sound the alarm by calling for Captain Willett, who was above decks in his cabin.

The raiders fired several more shots at Schaffer as he made his way toward the engine room, struggling to climb the ladder to the deck above. One found its mark and Schaffer fell dead, his body draped from the deck, half hanging down the ladder.

First Mate Charles Johnson, who had been joined by James Johnson, the first engineer, tried to lift the dead Schaffer off the ladder.

Mate Johnson turned and raced to Captain Willett's cabin. Firing excitedly, three of the engine room intruders chased after him. Responding to the sound of the shots and the scuffle on the deck, Willett opened his cabin door just as Johnson reached it. The mate, exclaiming Schaffer had been shot, dashed on to the pilot house, only to find it had been seized by the hijackers.

Johnson turned and darted out of the pilot house. Three of the men followed him. At the same time, two others came toward him from aft.

All five fired. Johnson was hit by two bullets; one lodged in his left arm and the other in his right knee. The marauders

George Wade wheeled and fired directly into Orin Schaffer's face.

continued to fire as Johnson stumbled to the cabin, but all the bullets missed. Joined by the first engineer, mate Johnson plunged into the engine room and was immediately fired upon by a man guarding the handcuffed Patrick Connor.

The kitchen lay ahead of them, but the only entrance from their side was through a small dumbwaiter in the bulkhead, which was used to pass food from the pantry to the cabin. Johnson helped the engineer, badly wounded in the chin during the melee, through the hole and then managed to force himself through the narrow opening.

Looking out a kitchen window, they saw a man they later learned was John Clibbon Brain, giving orders to three men who were throwing engineer Schaffer's body overboard. During this time the two Johnsons heard the sound of more shots being fired aboard the *Chesapeake*.

Just then the cook came into the kitchen to get his coat. The Johnsons asked if everyone else had been killed, to which the

the cook replied, "not all", whereupon they sent him to bring the man in charge of the attackers to the kitchen. Brain did not go himself, but his second in command, Henry Parr, went and told the men they were "... prisoners of the Southern Confederacy".

Parr took the two below where they found three men guarding the handcuffed captain, his son, two cabin boys, the cook, stewardess, and four passengers.

Captain Willett had been captured when he responded to mate Johnson's alarm that engineer Schaffer had been killed. Willett had been fired upon as he left his cabin and again as he stood over the dead engineer's body at the head of the engine room ladder. He had been shot at again as he turned and started toward the pilot house. Amazingly, all of the bullets missed.

As Willett stepped into the pilot house he was collared by Henry Parr, who shoved a pistol into his face and told him he was Parr's "prisoner in the name of the Southern Confederacy." A group of hijackers watched as Willett was handcuffed by Parr and escorted back to the cabin, where he found others of the *Chesapeake's* crew were being held prisoner.

Parr, who had once been a doctor, removed one lead ball from the first mate's arm, but was unable to cut the second out of his knee. He also tried, but failed, to remove a buried bullet from the chief engineer's chin.

Stewardess Mary Burgoyne, the only woman on board, had been in her room next to the engine room when she heard a volley of shots being fired. Peering out, she saw the first mate dash into the kitchen, followed by the first engineer. Quickly, she slammed her door shut.

Suddenly there was a knock on her door. Cautiously, she opened the door and peered into the darkness. It was the cook asking her if she were frightened. She answered "no" and asked if everyone else had been killed. "No," he replied, "but, we are prisoners to (sic) the Confederates ...".

Both Captain Willett and raider Henry Parr visited the young stewardess to reassure her. Later, Mary went to the kitchen and talked to George Robinson, the raider in charge of the deck. He told her not to be frightened, but proceeded to show her his revolver, which he claimed to have purchased in New York on Broadway.

Leaving Robinson, she crossed the deck to John Clibbon Brain's cabin. The hijackers' leader told her, "Don't be frightened, my wife gave me particular orders when I left home to take good care of you."

Mary had met Mrs. Brain when she accompanied Brain and Parr on their scouting mission aboard the *Chesapeake* a month earlier. Later, the raiders prepared a simple breakfast and fed the prisoners in small groups, allowing them to eat only while two armed men stood on either side of the table.

The *Chesapeake* was being navigated by Robert Osborne, a passenger pressed into service by Brain. Osborne had formerly captained the *Fellow Craft*, a small sailing vessel out of St. John. Brain also told James Johnson, the first engineer, to keep the engine room running smoothly.

The hijackers attempted to disguise the steamer by using paint from her stores to hide the *Chesapeake's* name and cover her distinctive yellow smoke stack stripe.

Clearly in command of his prize, Brain took the steamer's documents, including its coastal license, from Captain Willett. In return, he had Parr make a copy of his orders from Vernon Locke and give them to Willett.

Pistol in hand, Brain ordered Willett to return the eighty-seven dollars he had used to purchase the hijacker's tickets. Willett protested the funds belonged to the ship's owners, but eventually complied.

The hijackers seized eight revolvers in Willett's cabin and stole three of his coats. However, the captain was allowed to keep his clock, eight charts and his sextant.

The prisoners were allowed to roam the deck, but armed men were stationed on both sides of the steamer to watch them.

The *Chesapeake's* second mate, Daniel Henderson of Portland, overheard Brain and First Engineer James Johnson having a dispute over whether or not Orin Schaffer, the murdered second engineer, had been killed after he had fired a shot at the raiders. Brain insisted Schaffer must have fired the first shot. Johnson denied Schaffer had fired a pistol and said if Brain would allow it he would search the second engineer's room for Schaffer's pistol, which he usually kept in the bed. A search was made and the pistol was found in the cabin.

Brain later said his men had not fired at Schaffer until after the second engineer had fired three shots from a revolver.Brain also claimed Schaffer had been attempting to attach a hose to sweep the engine room deck with scalding water.

There is a possibility Schaffer had waved a cold water fire hose at the hijackers, pretending to scald them with hot water. Second Mate David Henderson later said:

> The second engineer might possibly get the apparatus for throwing hot water without help, but I doubt if he could, at all events he could not do it in less than twenty-five minutes. He would have first to go on deck from his engine room, then uncoil the hose from the hose box and extend it along the deck, then attach it to the goose neck on deck, then take it down to the engine room and put the machinery in motion ...

At night all the prisoners were ordered below. The officers were put in the cabin and the crew in the forecastle, except for the firemen, who were kept in the engine room to maintain steam in the boiler.

During the night the *Chesapeake* crossed Massachusetts Bay and entered the Gulf of Maine. Her first landfall was 1,530-foot-high Cadillac Mountain on Mount Desert Island. The Maine coastline remained on the off vessels's port side the rest of the day.

In reply to a series of insistent questions from Captain Willett, Brain indicated the *Chesapeake* would stop at Grand Manan Island, where the steamer's regular passengers would be put ashore. She would then proceed to St. John, approximately 100 miles up the coast.

Forty-six square-mile Grand Manan Island, which lies six miles at sea from West Quoddy Head, Maine, at the entrance to the Bay of Fundy, belongs to Canada's New Brunswick Province. It was the first neutral territory where Brain and his fellow hijackers could safely stop, either for refueling or to put Willett and his men ashore.

The *Chesapeake* reached Grand Manan's Seal Cove Harbor at seven o'clock Tuesday morning and Brain, pistol in hand, ordered David Henderson to let go the anchor.

London Illustrated News

The *Chesapeake* off Grand Manan Island.

After breakfast, a boat was lowered and Brain and three others went ashore for several hours before returning to their prize. Getting up steam again, the *Chesapeake* proceeded into the Bay of Fundy. A bark and a schooner were seen in the distance, one off to the east, the other off to the west.

The *Chesapeake* probed deeper into the Bay of Fundy. Late in the afternoon, Brain noticed a small pilot boat which had just put a pilot aboard an American ship bound for St. John Harbor.

Shortly thereafter the boat, which proved to be Mulherrin's *Pilot Boat No. 2*, out of St. John, drew alongside the larger *Chesapeake*. A small group of men had clustered on the *No. 2's* deck and one of them ordered Brain to stop the *Chesapeake*.

Brain apparently recognized someone on the small boat's deck because he immediately ordered his prize to stop. A man stepped from the group and climbed up over the *Chesapeake's* rail. He conferred with Brain several minutes before jumping back into the pilot boat. Several minutes later Captain Vernon Locke, alais Captain John Parker of the former Confederate privateer *Retribution*, who a week previously had ordered Brain to seize a steamer, heaved a valise over the rail and scampered after it.

Quickly assuming command, Locke ordered the pilot boat taken in tow and commanded the helmsman to head the *Chesapeake* toward Dipper Harbor on the nearby New Brunswick shore.

Drawing abreast of Partridge Island, which lies outside St. John Harbor, the *Chesapeake* hove to while Locke, Brain and several others rowed ashore in a small boat. The steamer remained off the island about three hours until Locke and Brain returned, and the vessel again headed down east.

Later, the pilot boat was brought alongside and Locke ordered Captain Willett and most of his crew into it. Five passengers were allowed to join them, but Robert Osborne, the ill-fated passenger who had been piloting the ship, was ordered to stay on board, as were engineers James Johnson and Augustus Starbeck, and three firemen, who were needed to keep the engine running.

At eight o'clock in the evening, after towing the pilot boat another three miles, Locke ordered the tow line cast off and

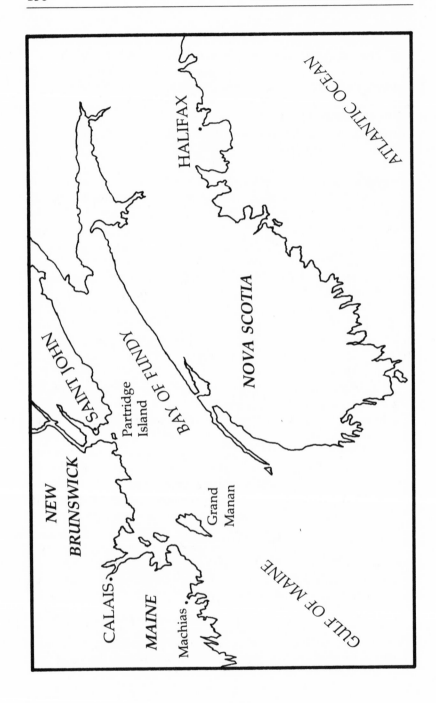

the prisoners were freed. The *Chesapeake* steamed off in the darkness toward the distant Nova Scotia shore.

Hours later, near Partridge Island, Captain Willett hailed a large ship and convinced her captain to loan him a better boat to reach St. John. Willett, some of his crew and the five passengers, finally arrived in St. John at four o'clock in the morning on Wednesday, December 9th. The rest of *Chesapeake's* crew arrived later that morning aboard the pilot boat.

United States Consul J. Q. Howard, arriving at his office to begin his day as the State Department's representative in St. John, found Captain Isaac Willett waiting for him. Soon the wires were humming with telegrams from Howard to his superiors in Washington and to officials in Portland, where the *Chesapeake* had been bound.

Howard's terse telegram to the Portland Merchant's Exchange said:

> The second mate of the *Chesapeake* shot dead, his body thrown overboard. Chief Engineer shot in the chin, but retained on board. First mate badly wounded in the groin. Eleven or twelve shots fired at the Captain. After being overpowered the Captain was put in irons and the crew notified they were prisoners of war of the Confederate States of America

Alerted by Howard's messages, Secretary of the Navy Gideon Welles dispatched a series of telegrams to naval bases in the northeast, ordering their commanders to dispatch all available vessels after the *Chesapeake*. The Navy responded rapidly, and at four o'clock that same afternoon the *U.S.S. Acacia* steamed out of the Boston Navy Yard in pursuit of John Clibbon Brain and the *Chesapeake*.

CHAPTER FOURTEEN

THE CHESAPEAKE RECAPTURED

The United States Navy's search for the elusive *Chesapeake* swung into full force on December 10, 1863. All along the northeast coast, Federal vessels were readied and sent to sea after Brain and his prize.

In Portland, the *U.S.S. Agawam* sailed, minus her captain, who was sick at home. At the Boston Navy Yard, the vessel *Ella & Annie* was manned and armed, then steamed out of Boston Harbor at 1:40 P.M.

The Ella & Annie was commanded by Lt. J. F. Nickels of Searsport, Maine. When the war began, Nickels was a part-owner and master of a merchant vessel which was then at sea. He left the ship as soon as it reached an American port to enlist in the Navy. His first brief command was the *U.S.S. Onward*. He was soon given charge of the *U.S.S. Cherokee*, a steamer being outfitted in Boston. Learning of the *Chesapeake's* capture, Nickels insisted he be allowed to help down the hijackers and was subsequently put in command of the *Ella & Annie*, later named the *U.S.S. Malvern*.

Secretary of the Navy Gideon Welles wired Admiral Paulding, commander of the New York Navy Yard, to send any available steamer after the *Chesapeake*, but cautioned him not to charter any vessels for this purpose.

The H. B. Cromwell Company, the *Chesapeake's* owners, wired Welles offering two vessels to assist the search. Ultimately they could only provide the steamer a single steamer, which Welles later declined on the grounds that several armed vessels were already in pursuit of the *Chesapeake*.

A security scheme based on the use of a special pass system was quickly established in New York Harbor. No vessel could leave without a pass from the U.S. Marshal and all passengers had to submit to both a personal inspection and a thorough check of all their baggage.

During all this activity Vernon Locke and John Clibbon Brain had steamed the *Chesapeake* out of the Bay of Fundy around the tip of Cape Sable to the tiny port of Shelburne, on the mouth of the Roseway River in southwestern Nova Scotia.

The *Chesapeake* arrived in Shelburne Harbor at nine P.M. December 10th. Her passage had not been an easy one. Vernon Locke had told those aboard he was a native of the area and decided to act as his own pilot. Enroute, the steamer fought constant rough weather, struggling through both a snowstorm and a heavy gale off Cape Sable.

Two miles from Shelburne, the *Chesapeake* stopped and let go her anchor. The hijackers reported the vessel's arrival at the Custom House and said their ship was the steamer *Jane*, Captain George Parker commanding, from Wilmington, N.C., bound for Bermuda via Halifax with an assorted cargo.

Cornelius White, the U.S. Consular Agent in Shelburne immediately dispatched a wire to his superiors at the consulate in Halifax reporting the vessel's arrival. White indicated the steamer had not displayed a trail board bearing her name and said he believed Vernon Locke of the *Retribution* was in command.

The hijackers arranged to obtain some soft coal and about two cords of wood from a schooner in the harbor. The vessel's crew was given some of the *Chesapeake's* freight in payment. In addition, a Nova Scotian named Kenny bought more than a $1,000 worth of flour, sugar, tobacco, and port wine from the hijackers, who apparently had few scruples about selling their prize's cargo.

In peddling the steamer's cargo, Locke and Brain were in violation of Nova Scotia's revenue laws. As such they had divested themselves of the character of officers engaged in legitimate warfare. Brain abruptly left the vessel at Shelburne, and four other men, all Nova Scotians, were hired to join the crew.

Shortly afterwards, the *Chesapeake* steamed east from Shelburne Harbor. Off to the westward, in the Gulf of Maine, the Federal pursuit of the *Chesapeake* had been plagued by both bad luck and inclement weather. The *U.S.S Acacia*, which had raced from Boston, was forced to scurry into Portland Harbor after continued violent pounding by angry seas opened several of her seams. Her captain reported to the Portsmouth Navy Yard that only the timely arrival of several fire department pumps had kept his warship afloat at a Portland dock.

The *U.S.S. Ticonderoga* sailed from New York at 10 A.M. December 11th in favorable weather. By midnight a snowstorm had set in and lasted for ten hours. The snow was followed by a dense fog, which plagued the vessel until midnight on the 14th.

On the evening of the thirteenth, a strong southeast blow sprang up, gradually veering to the south and then west before increasing to a whole gale that stirred up mountainous seas. The high winds continued for more than twenty-four hours.

On the morning of the sixteenth the weather cleared. Using his sextant for the first time in four days, a dismayed Captain Charles Steedman calculated that his ship had been blown more than 200 miles to the southward. He decided to abandon his pursuit on the grounds his quarry had probably already fled Nova Scotian waters.

In spite of the terrible weather, the Navy, urged on by Secretary Welles, continued to send vessels after the *Chesapeake*. In Gloucester, Massachusetts, Thomas T. Craven, commander of the *U.S.S. Niagara*, closed out his ship's accounts, obtained a harbor pilot, and hoisted his anchor to chase after the elusive quarry.

Hampered by easterly winds, a head sea and heavy fog, the *Niagara* labored more then forty-eight hours to make the passage from Gloucester to the Nova Scotian littoral. Communicating with those ashore shore, Captain Craven was unable to learn any information about the *Chesapeake*. He then spent the next eighty-five hours on the lee shore riding out a stubborn gale. Speaking with the shore again, he learned that a steamer matching the *Chesapeake's* description had "passed by Yarmouth on the 12th instant steering southward..." A telegram informed Craven his quarry was at La Have River, being blockaded by a Federal gunboat. The *Niagara* immediately got under way for the intended rendezvous.

Avoiding his Union Navy pursuers, Locke had defied the weather and taken the *Chesapeake* to La Have River, which ran inland almost to the town of Bridgewater, halfway between Shelburne and Halifax.

The *Chesapeake* had left Shelburne Friday morning, December 11th. Enroute, its crew of hijackers spotted a steamer working through the storm. The steamer was the *Ella & Annie*, which had arrived at Eastport, Maine on December 12th, leaving an hour when her skipper, Captain Nickels, received word the *Chesapeake* had been seen in the vicinity of St. Margaret's Bay, across a wide peninsula from Halifax.

The *Chesapeake* hugged the shoreline the rest of the day and then ascended the La Have late at night. The hijackers remained four days on the upper river while they sold a considerable amount of the ship's cargo, especially flour, sugar, port wine, tobacco and cotton, to local citizens.

Astoundingly, the *Chesapeake* had been cleared to enter the La Have by the Collector of Customs of nearby Lunenburg. The vessel was admitted as the *Retribution*, a Confederate war vessel. Brain, who rejoined the vessel at Lunenburg, had produced his commission at the collector's request, after which then he and several others were permitted to land and sell some of the steamer's cargo in order to obtain necessary supplies.

At New Dublin, Brain sold several cases of stationery and some bales of leather in return for provisions. However, as soon as the collector realized what he had done, he prohibited the landing of any additional cargo until he received proper authority from his superiors.

A month later, while reading in the newspaper about Locke's accomplishments with the *Chesapeake* at La Have River, the Reverend John H. Drum of Bristol, Pennsylvania, formerly a chaplain in the U.S. Volunteers, penned a letter to President Lincoln:

> From a long residence on the coast of Nova Scotia I felt convinced as soon as the first reports reached us, that no Southerner could have known so well where to bring the vessel, what harbors to seek, what to avoid, and where to find and seek a market for the cargo, and at last I was assured by the mention of the Captain's name that the chief actors in the affair were Nova Scotians.
>
> The "Captain" is named "Locke". There is a man of that name, (owner of one or more coasters or small vessels trading to West Indies) who resides at the Ragged Islands, near Shelburne, N.S. His family rule in that vicinity. They trade a good deal and possibly smuggle a good deal; one member is a representative in the Colonial Legislature. Shelburne, near the Ragged Islands, has one of the finest harbors in the world, but it is little known and less used, there being but little trade in that section of the country.
>
> Whither then the *Chesapeake* was taken first for security and privacy, but it was not designed to dispose of her cargo there (and indeed was not possible) she was immediately taken to La Have River near Lunenburg. On that river, about 15 miles from the mouth, lives an Irishman Mr. Wm. McKean, who is an extensive trader, & always has a large amount of cash on hand, and is always ready to go into a profitable speculation without being fastidious as to its full legality or equity. No other man I venture to say between Yarmouth & Halifax could have bought the cargo of the *Chesapeake* for cash & this is a fact not very well known even in Halifax. Yet right to his door the *Chesapeake* was brought. ... I venture unhestitatingly to assert that Wm. McKean of "Conquer all Bank", La Have River was the chief purchaser.
>
> ... Captain Locke is an intimate friend of McKean's and has sailed in his employ.
>
> No vessel of the same size I fancy, certainly no steamer, has ever before been up the La Have river but this one under the charge of Captain Locke is taken up there to the front of Mr. Wm. Mc Kean's house and the flour sold at 3.00 a barrel and sugar at 3 cents a pound ! to personal friends of a Captain Locke who is a British subject & holds no commission under the so called "Confederate Authorities".

John Clibbon Brain, left the vessel while it was at La Have, taking a box containing $400 worth of jewelry with him. Fellow hijacker Parr told James Johnson, the *Chesapeake's* captive First Engineer, that Brain was "behaving badly" and that he, Parr, was going after him. Parr left the steamer and did not return.

Brain, who was enroute to Halifax, was arrested by the provincial authorities in Liverpool. However, the wily swindler-hijacker swiftly produced his fraudulant papers and was allowed to go free, much to the consternation of the United States vice consul, who had instigated the arrest.

Offshore, the search for the hijackers and their prize was continuing as the Navy continued to send vessels after the *Chesapeake*. On December 12th, while the ships already at sea were groping through a murky fog bank surrounding the Nova Scotia coast, the *U.S.S. Dacotah* slid down the Piscatataqua River from the Portsmouth Navy Yard and headed across the Gulf of Maine toward the Maritimes. She was followed on the sixteenth by the steamer *Cornubia*, out of the Charlestown Navy Yard.

The *Dacotah* sailed short-handed and her crew complemented with sailors from the Portsmouth receiving ship. Her orders were to search the Nova Scotia coast off Cape Sable. Captain A. G. Clary, her commander, was told to demand the *Chesapeake* from the local authorities if the steamer were found in a Nova Scotian port.

The *Dacotah's* pursuit of the *Chesapeake* was slowed by two days of heavy weather. On the fourteenth, Captain Clary spoke with the American ship *Argo*, out of St. John. The *Argo's* captain reported the *Chesapeake* had left that port on the ninth, bound east.

Clary, acting on both this information and a series of telegrams he had received prior to sailing, headed for Shelburne, where he arrived on the fifteenth, only to discover his quarry had left there three days earlier.

Resorting to the telegraph to track the *Chesapeake's* passage along the coast, Clary received word the steamer lay at La Have, sixty miles further east. Pushing on, the *Dacotah* reached La Have at 5 P.M. on the sixteenth, only to learn from the port's lighthouse keeper that the *Chesapeake* had steamed away to the eastward.

Meanwhile, the *Ella & Annie*, the command of Lieutenant Nickels, arrived off Cross Island, at the entrance to St. Margaret's Bay, at 6 P.M. December thirteenth. However, the weather was so thick the warship could not to enter the bay. Fog, combined with a heavy blow from the south, prevented the vessel from sighting land again until 2 P. M. on the fifteeenth. Lieutenant Nickels was discouraged to find his command had been pushed well east of the bay.

Returning to St. Margaret's Bay where it was assumed their quarry was hiding, the *Ella & Annie* was unable to enter. Lieutenant Nickels had almost exhausted his supply of coal while attempting to maintain his position in the storm and the greatly lightened vessel was being badly mauled by the stormy seas.

Nickels turned the *Ella & Annie* about and ran for Halifax, where the Union warship drew alongside the Cunard coaling wharf at 5:30 P.M.

Five-and-a-half hours later, having loaded 136 tons of coal, the *Ella & Annie* steamed from Halifax Harbor for La Have River, where the *Chesapeake* was reported hiding.

A strong westerly gale had been blowing and the *Ella & Annie* had difficulty making windward way. A tired but a determined Lieutenant Nickels finally edged his ship into La Have at 3 o'clock the following afternoon only to be told the *Chesapeake* had slipped from the harbor the night before and had cleared the river's mouth that very morning.

Actually, the *Chesapeake* had steamed from La Have early that morning for St. Margaret's Bay. At 9 A.M. the *Chesapeake's* lookout spotted a steamer, probably the *Ella & Annie*, which Locke eluded by having his vessel hug the shore. By early afternoon the *Chesapeake* was off Sambro where a pilot named Flynn came aboard and guided her into the harbor.

Worried by the sad state of the *Chesapeake's*'s dwindling coal supply, Locke left immediately for Halifax. Twelve hours later he returned aboard the British sloop *Investigator*, Captain John E. Holt commanding, with a supply of coal. Also aboard were John Fleming, a Halifax Harbor pilot; and George Tanner, Master Mariner; two engineers and two firemen, Nova Scotians Locke had hired in Halifax to assist in manning the *Chesapeake's* engines.

Captain Nickels of the *Ella & Annie* had been told at La Have the *Chesapeake* Might be at Lunenburg, the next bay to the eastward. With her nearly exhausted stokers pouring on the coal, the *Ella & Annie* steamed out of the La Have River and arrived at Lunenburg at 6:30 in the evening.

The same day, Wednesday, December 16th, hijacker Henry Parr left the *Chesapeake* at La Have, and went to Lunenburg to try and purchase coal from a schooner anchored in the harbor. In Lunenburg he went to the post office to wire Halifax seeking more fuel for the *Chesapeake*.

At the post office, Parr did not seem to be in any great hurry and spent time talking to Mrs. Rudolph, the post mistress, while the *Ella & Annie* appeared and anchored just offshore.

Captain Nickels, who had no idea one of the hijackers was in town, came ashore to send a series of telegrams seeking reports of the *Chesapeake's* location from the authorities of the ports and small harbors along the neighboring coast.

Striding to the post office, he found a locked door. He knocked and Mrs. Rudolph peeked out, surprised to see a man dressed in a naval uniform. Thinking quickly, she pulled the curtain down and hustled Parr into another room before admitting Nickels.

The Ella & Annie's commander fired off a telegram to Halifax asking the *Chesapeake's* last location. A momentary reply revealed his quarry was even then at Mud Cove, Sambro Harbor, near the approach to Halifax Harbor. Hurrying back to his vessel, Nickels headed the *Ella & Annie* out of Lunenburg Harbor and steamed for Sambro.

The *Ella & Annie* soon reached Sambro, but had to heave to at the harbor's mouth to await a local pilot. At daylight, the warship got up steam and started into the harbor, hoping to capture the *Chesapeake* while the hijackers were still asleep and off guard. Captain Nickels spotted the *Chesapeake* in the inner harbor with a schooner tied alongside.

Nickels ordered the *Ella & Annie's* decks cleared for action and ran out the warship's starboard guns. In clear violation of British neutrality, the United States warship charged into the inner harbor.

Throughout the previous night, the *Chesapeake* had been re-coaling. About 2 A.M., Captain Locke had asked James

The U.S.S. *Malvern*, previously the *Ella & Annie*.

Johnson, the steamer's captive first engineer, to show the engine room and its machinery to the engineers who had arrived aboard the *Investigator*. Locke also told Johnson he would be free to leave in the morning. Johnson replied he would show the engineers the engine room at daylight.

Eager to be freed, Johnson briefed the new engineers on the *Chesapeake's* engine and its idiosyncrasies the first thing the next morning. He then went to his stateroom to pack and leave the steamer.

Pilot Flynn, who had brought the *Chesapeake* into Sambro the day before, was the first to see the *Ella & Annie* steaming into the harbor. Scurrying below, he reported the sighting to Vernon Locke, who scrambled on deck and screamed at his new engineer to get up steam. The Nova Scotian replied that he and his men could not do so on such short notice.

Locke returned below decks where James Johnson was preparing to go ashore. He asked the former engineer to scuttle the *Chesapeake*. Johnson refused, saying he did not know how. Locke suggested he cut a pipe to scuttle the ship, to which Johnson replied there weren't any he could cut.

Foiled in his attempt to sink his prize, Locke returned on deck, where he ordered his crew of hijackers to abandon the *Chesapeake* and flee.

Engineer Johnson, clothing in hand, arrived topside a minute or two later to find Locke and the others pulling away in a small boat. Johnson, sighting the warship heading directly toward the *Chesapeake*, ran to the wheelhouse where he located an American flag, which he had a fireman run up the steamer's mast with the union upside down.

Aboard the *Investigator*, Captain Holt, alerted by the frantic activity aboard the *Chesapeake*, quickly ordered the lines cast off that connected the two craft.

The *Investigator* then moved further up the harbor and anchored approximately 400 yards from the *Chesapeake* and 200 yards from the shore.

Meanwhile, aboard the *Ella & Annie*, Lieutenant Nickels noticed the American flag, union down, flying from the *Chesapeake's* mast. In his eagerness to come alongside the latter vessel, Nickels ran his ship into the steamer's port bow, before he finally slowed his vessel and warped her alongside the *Chesapeake's* starboard side.

An eager prize crew from the *Ella & Annie* swarmed over the steamer's side. Their charge went unresisted and they soon realized the *Chesapeake's* hijackers had all fled in the small boat, which they had seen as the *Ella & Annie* entered the harbor.

The boarding party did discover seven men aboard the recaptured steamer. Four of them, three firemen and an oiler, were members of the *Chesapeake's* original crew. Two others were engineers brought aboard by Locke, who were subsequently left behind when the hijackers fled. The seventh man was First Engineer James Johnson.

The two Nova Scotians were arrested and placed in irons.

A prize crew was put aboard the *Chesapeake* and the men finished recoaling the steamer from the *Ella & Annie's* supply and began provisioning their prize prior to setting out for an American port.

An armed boat's crew consisting of an officer and seven men was sent aboard the *Investigator*. Their arrival was challenged by Captian Holt, who asked the boat's officer to show his authority for boarding a neutral British schooner. The officer replied by striking his pistol with his hand and saying, "This is my authority!" Holt protested, but ceased when three of the *Ella & Annie's* men cocked their weapons and ordered him to hold his tongue.

The American crew then took possession of the *Investigator* and searched it from stem to stern, keeping an armed guard on deck at all times.

The *Ella & Annie's* party found George Wade, the hijacker who had murdered Second Engineer Schaffer, attempting to hide under a buffalo robe in the schooner's cabin. He was taken aboard the *Ella & Annie*, and placed in double irons, joining the two Nova Scotians who had been similarly shackled after their capture during the *Chesapeake's* boarding.

The Federal crew also found several large packages and trunks which had been taken by the *Chesapeake*. These they transferred to the *Ella & Annie*, preparatory to her return to Boston.

The *Ella & Annie* had entered Sambro Harbor around 8 A.M. and by early afternoon Captain Nickels and his crew had recaptured the *Chesapeake*, boarded and searched the

Investigator, and re-coaled the former vessel. Acting Master William McGlown was placed in charge of the steamer and ordered to proceed to Boston, and report to the commandant of the Boston Navy Yard.

That afternoon the *Ella & Annie* and the *Chesapeake* steamed out of Sambro. At the harbor's mouth they were met by the *U.S.S. Dacotah*, Captain Clary commanding. Clary hailed the *Ella & Annie* and asked if the other vessel was the *Chesapeake*. A proud Lieutenant Nickels replied in the affirmative. Clary then asked where the steamer was being taken. Nickels answered, "Boston."

The *Dacotah's* captain inquired if any of the "pirates" had been captured. When Nickels shouted back that he had taken three of the hijackers, Clary, who was the senior officer present, ordered Nickels to join him aboard the *Dacotah*.

Forseeing diplomatic problems arising from the *Chesapeake's* recapture in a neutral harbor, Clary ordered Nickels to take the steamer to Halifax for adjudication. Nickels obeyed and the *Ella & Annie* accompanied the *Chesapeake* to Halifax, where both vessels anchored at 3:45 P.M. The *Dacotah* arrived fifteen minutes later.

Captain Clary quickly immediately communicated with both the U. S. Consul and the provincial authorities regarding the *Chesapeake's* recapture and sent a telegram reporting the *Ella & Annie's* success to Secretary of the Navy Gideon Welles.

The next morning, December 18th, Clary received a reply from Welles ordering him to turn the *Chesapeake* over to the Nova Scotian provincial authorities.

The Nova Scotian authorities were well aware that three Federal naval vessels had anchored in Halifax Harbor, along with the *Chesapeake*. Provincial Secretary Charles Tupper sent Clary a stiff note asking: "... the names of the ships under your command, the object of your visit to this port, and the circumstances under which the steamship *Chesapeake* has been this day taken out of the harbor of Sambro, a Nova Scotia port, and brought into this harbor by men-of-war belonging to the Navy of the United States."

Clary, in a tongue-in-cheek reply wrote:

At 7 o'clock this morning a flag of distress of the United States was seen flying by the crew of the U.S. gunboat *Ella & Annie*, under the command of Acting Lieutenant J. F. Nickels, the *Ella & Annie* steaming into Sambro in order to grant relief to such signal from a vessel purporting to belong to the United States. When Acting Lieutenant Nickels reached the distressed [vessel] he found her to be the the the steamboat *Chesapeake*, in possession and control of five of her original crew, by whom he was informed that the piraytes had abandoned her and that the *Chesapeake* was without fuel. Under the circumstances of the case I thought it prudent to put into the port of Halifax for the purpose of puting myself in communication with the British authorities and the U. S. Government.

Clary and the provincial authorities exchanged a series of letters and it was finally arranged for Clary to turn the *Chesapeake* over to Captain O'Brien of the revenue schooner *Daring* on the afternoon of December 19th. The return of the *Chesapeake* was to be preceded by Clary turning hijacker George Wade and the two Nova Scotian engineers over to to J. J. Lawyer, high sheriff of the County of Halifax, at Queen's Wharf.

Agreeing to both exchanges, Clary dispatched a small boat containing Ensign Coughlin of the *Ella & Annie* and the three prisoners, still in double irons, to Queen's Wharf.

A delegation of officials, including Provincial Secretary Charles Tupper, Solicitor General W. A. Henry, and High Sheriff J. J. Sawyer, had assembled on the wharf, together with several police officers and a group of interested citizens, including Dr. W. J. Almon, a strong pro-Southern Nova Scotian.

U.S. Consul Nathaniel Gunnison was also waiting for the prisoners to be brought ashore. Gunnison had obtained a warrant, good only within the Halifax city limits, for Wade's arrest for the murder of Schaffer, the *Chesapeake's* second engineer. Lewis Hutt, a Halifax city constable, was assigned to actually serve the warrant and arrest Wade. However, Hutt was late and did not arrive at the wharf until the prisoners had been brought ashore.

At Queen's Wharf, Ensign Coghlan turned his prisoners over to Sheriff Sawyer, who demanded the trio be unshackled. Coghlan unlocked the irons and the sheriff, after ascertaining the prisoners names, told the men they were at liberty to leave as free men.

At that moment, Dr. Almon stepped forward from the crowd to shake the hand of one of the former prisoners, an engineer by the name of Henry, who was well known in Halifax. While everyone in Henry's immediate vicinity was being distracted by Dr. Almon's greeting, a small rowboat manned by two strong-armed fishermen named Holland and Gallagher slid alongside the wharf.

Suddenly, Almon wheeled and whispered in Wade's ear. Almost instantly Wade turned and jumped into the fishermen's rowboat, which quickly pulled away from the wharf and slid between the *Dacotah's* small boat and a schooner on the other side. The crowd cheered as a few more strokes by Holland and Gallagher propelled the rowboat into clear water.

At this moment a late constable Hutt arrived at the wharf to see his quarry slipping away as the crowd hollared its approval. Dressed in civilan clothes and showing no badge of authority, Hutt rushed down the wharf yelling "Stop, stop!". As the boat continued its getaway Hutt drew and leveled his pistol, shouting that he would fire unless the boat stopped.

Dr. Almon seized Hutt's gun arm and the two tumbled into the water. As the rowboat rounded the wharf's end, Wade shouted three times to the crowd, "For God's sake, thank the Queen for my liberty!"

Holland and Gallagher rowed Wade to nearby Ketch Harbor, where he was given a fast horse to escape the province. Dr. Almon and two others were later brought to trial for helping Wade escape. All three were released with a reprimand, although Dr. Almon was required to pay a small fine.

Three of the original *Chesapeake* raiders, David Collins, James McKinney, and Linus Seely, who had made their way back to New Brunswick after escaping at Sambro, were arrested outside St. John and brought to trial in that city. The trio were actually subjected to two trials. The first, at the police magistrate's court, resulted in Collins, McKinney and Seely being found guilty on the grounds the *Chesapeake's* hijacking was an act of piracy, rather than an act of war. The three were ordered to be held in jail at St. John until extradition to the United States could be arranged.

However, no one was ever extradited, as their defense lawyer appealed the original court's finding and took their case to a higher court. On March 10, 1864, Judge W.J. Ritchie ruled the three should be discharged because the warrant for their arrest had been defective. He also found that the alleged crime of piracy had occurred under United States jurisdiction and that the legal proceedings should have taken place in the United States.

The other *Chesapeake* raiders were never captured. A warrant for Brain's arrest had been issued in Halifax while the *Chesapeake* was steaming from LaHave to its final port at Sambro. Two Halifax city constables and a Halifax county officer traveled to Sambro on the day the hijackers abandoned their prize.

They arrived to find the men, minus Brain, who had left the steamer previously, parading around the streets of the small town in a tight group. The group brandished their revolvers and fired a few shots into the air to intimidate the policemen, who decided there would be bloodshed if they attempted to arrest the hijackers. Out numbered twelve to three, the lawmen retreated to Halifax.

The outlaws scattered, some travelling to Halifax while others scurried elsewhere. Vernon Locke rode to Halifax in a carriage driven by his brother Eben Locke, who had arrived in Sambro a half-hour after the Federal forces left there with the *Chesapeake*.

Meanwhile, the elusive John Clibbon Brain continued to elude the authorities who were seeking to enforce the warrant for his arrest. Leaving Nova Scotia, Brain returned to St. John where the whole adventure had begin less than a month previously.

The St. John *Daily Telegraph,* on December 24, 1863, reported Brain had been staying at the St. Lawrence Hotel. The paper stated, "Lieut. Braine takes matters easily, calling at hat stores and photographic saloons, and in other ways improving his time while here."

However, the police were hot on Brain's trail and he was forced to leave left St. John and return to Halifax, where he caught a ship for Bermuda. Brain passed through Moncton with two St. John policemen close behind him. At Dorcester the police where told Brain had just left for Amherst, Nova Scotia. They chased off to Sackville, on the New Brunswick - Nova Scotia border, only to learn he was still at Dorcester. The *Daily Telegraph* commented, "They are quite confiding and utterly unfit for duty for which they have been detailed. The Lt. is probably in Halifax."

The authorities in Truro, on the main line from Moncton, telegraphed Halifax reporting Brain was headed for that city. They requested a military force be sent to the Richmond Station to assist the police in arresting Brain when his train arrived there. One hundred soldiers were rushed to Richmond Station and surrounded the arriving train, only to find Brain was not in any of the cars.

It is not known how Brain eluded the military force, but he was later seen getting off a train at Bedford Station, which is at the end of the Bedford Basin, ten-and-a-half miles above Halifax. He was apparently making for Hammond Plains and St. Margaret's Bay, where he could hide out while still being able to communicate with friends in Halifax. The press, reporting Brain's escape, commented: "... unless we mistake the sagacity of our constabulary here a strong force will be on its way to the place in question, and Braine will be a lucky man indeed if he escapes their clutches."

John Clibbon Brain, the swindler, spy, and ship hijacker, eluded his pursuers and eventually boarded a ship for Bermuda. By March of 1864, he had successfully ran the blockade to Wilmington. He would be heard from again along the eastern seaboard. Before the war was over and before he could be brought before the bar of justice for his part in the *Chesapeake's* hijacking, he successfully hijacked two more vessels.

CHAPTER FIFTEEN

BRAIN STRIKES AGAIN

John Clibbon Brain continued to plague the United States Navy for several years and and to confound police officials and hotel keepers across the South for years after the Civil War.

On May 26, 1864, he was appointed an Acting Master in the Confederate States Navy by Stephen R. Mallory, Secretary of the Navy. Brain's letter of appointment also outlined the new Acting Master's orders:

> Herewith you will receive an appointment of acting master in the Navy, and will proceed to Wilmington, and there make the necessary arrangements to capture upon the high seas the Federal steamer *Roanoke*, or the steamers *Morning [Star]* or *Evening Star*, all of which vessels are on a line running between New York and Havana.
>
> In case you succeed in capturing either of the above steamers you will bring her and the prisoners of war into a Confederate port.
>
> The strictest regard for the rights of neutrals and neutral property must be observed, and the discipline and subordination preserved among officers and men under your command as a measure of security and success.

Brain was authorized to appoint three Master's Mates and three Acting Third Engineers and was told to report their names to the Navy Department.

John Clibbon Brain was back in the ship-hijacking business!

At the time of his appointment, Brain was the leader of a group Wilmington men who wanted to obtain a letter of marque like the one Vernon Locke had possessed when he commanded the *Retribution*.

According to J.P. Benjamin, Confederate Secretary of State, Brain had requested an appointment as an Acting Master in the Confederate Navy as a means of protection if he were captured. He wanted to be able to prove his actions had official sanction, rather than being those of a common pirate.

Although Brain and his men lacked a ship, the former spy and swindler proposed to solve that problem by going to New York through the Union lines, then taking passage on a steamer bound to Havana and capturing her while on the high seas.

Brain later claimed he had presented his case to both President Jefferson Davis and to Secretary of the Navy Mallory. It is doubtful he ever talked to or actually had an appointment with the president. Secretary Mallory, in appointing Brain an Acting Master, admonished him to have the "strictest regard for the rights of neutrals and neutral property."

Brain's pardon file in the National Archives includes a fascinating copy of an undated invoice sent to his lawyer by one of Brain's former crewmen, who was living in Texas at the time. The invoice, written on the usual yellow or gray paper used by the Confederates, was for ordnance stores issued to Brain by Lt. R. O. Minor, commander of the New Orleans ordnance factory. It indicated Brain was being issued 6 LeMats revolvers, 250 ball cartridges, 50 buckshot, 300 percussion caps, and six cutlasses and scabbards.

There are apparently no existing records of the names and backgrounds of the crew Brain assembled. However, diplomatic and press reports of the hijacking of Brain's target, the mail steamer *Roanoke*, reveal one of his chief assistants was Henry Parr, who had played a prominent part in the capture of the *Chesapeake* the previous year.

Brain and his men traveled to Bermuda, probably by taking a blockade runner from Wilmington. In Bermuda he purchased a schooner and cleared for Matanzas, in northern Cuba. Enroute, however, he detoured to Nassau in the Bahamas and the cruise to Matanzas took forty days.

From Matanzas, Brain traveled to Havana where he called on Charles J. Helm, the resident Confederate agent. The new Acting Master told Helm he needed $1,500 to carry out his plot to seize a Union vessel. Brain said he had received $3,000 from Secretary of the Navy Mallory and another $1,000 from the Confederate agent in Nassau.

Brain told Helm his schooner was old, unseaworthy, and unsailable, and that he had come to Havana to obtain $1,500, recruit ten reliable men, and purchase arms and handcuffs.

He showed the agent his is orders from Secretary Mallory and insisted he had received verbal orders from both Mallory and President Davis to make his attempt from Havana.

Helm was not fooled by the former swindler's gambit. Forcefully, he told Brain that the plan to embark from Havana and seize a vessel would be considered an "unjustifiable interference" with Spanish neutrality by the authorities in Havana. He also warned Brain his that plot, if successful, would be "greatly prejudicial" to the interests of the Confederacy.

But, Brain was not ready to give up his attempt to obtain funds from Helm. He immediately sent the Confederate agent a letter asking for a loan.

> Havana, [August] 12, 1864
> Sir: I have received certain orders from the Secretary of the Navy of the Confederate States (a copy of which orders I herewith send), but it will be utterly impossible for me to execute them unless I am provided with a sufficient amount of funds. I will need at least $1,500. As agent of the Confederate States, you are the only one that I can, with any propriety, apply to for said funds, and I therefore respectfully ask you in the name of our Government to lend me your valuable aid in this emergency.

Helm replied four days later, rejecting Brain's appeal. In his reply, Helm reiterated his stand that Brain's proposal would violate Spanish neutrality and proclaimed he would assume full responsibility for foiling the plan.

> ... Had I the funds I should still decline to aid you in embarking with your party from the neutral port of Havana for the purpose of capturing one of the enemy's ships, as such an act would be a violation of the respect due to neutral territory not contemplated by your order ... I shall of course explain very fully to the Government my reason for preventing an act which

> I believe would lead to unpleasant complications with the
> Spanish government, not desired by the Confederacy, and will
> assume all responsibility in the matter, by which you will be
> entirely relieved from blame, even should the President and
> Secretary of the Navy decide that my judgement and
> conception of the law is at fault.

Helm immediately reported his action to Secretary of State
Judah P. Benjamin in Richmond. Benjamin checked Brain's
status with the Navy Department and then replied:

> ... In relation to the affair of Braine, you were not mistaken in
> the inference that he was unworthy of credit in his statements
> to you. He never saw the President, and of course had no such
> conversation with him as Braine reported to you. ... The
> attempt of Braine to organize a hostile expedition in the harbor
> of Havana was a gross outrage, and you very property
> prevented its accomplishment.

Benjamin's letter was written September 13th and reached
Helm in Havana October 17th, together with other mail which
brought news of the hijacking of the steamer *Roanoke* by John
Clibbon Brain. Both Helm and Benjamin had underestimated
estimated Brain's determination to seize a vessel outward
bound from Havana.

Helm had even gone so far as to convince twelve of Brain's
crew, who said they were destitute, to abandon the enterprise
and return home. On August 23rd, after Brain refused to pay
their board, Helm booked passage for the dozen on a ship
bound for Nassau. The men had no landing permits and could
not obtain passports, which were necessary to board a ship
leaving Havana. Helm went to the office of Brigadier-General
Perry, the port captain, and told Perry why the men were in
Havana and why he was sending them home. Perry
immediately granted them permission to leave and they
sailed at once on the British schooner *Wild Pigeon*.

Brain, who had assumed an alias and was calling himself
Johnson, remained behind. He spent part of his time
attempting to sell a draft on the account of C. J. McRae, the
Confederate agent in Paris. Helm saw Brain in the streets
several times, but the captor of the *Chesapeake* never again
approached him for funds or any other assistance.

Brain found himself in Havana with only one friend, Henry Parr, who had been one of his lieutenants in the *Chesapeake* affair. However, the glib-tongued Brain quickly recruited eight men to replace those Helm had sent home, and again began plotting to seize the *Roanoke*.

On September 29, 1864, the mail steamer *Roanoke*, with Captain Francis A. Drew in command, left Havana bound for New York. She passed Morro Castle at 5 P.M. with twenty-four cabin and sixteen steerage passengers, plus fifty officers and crew aboard.   Steamers such as the *Roanake* did not tie up at a wharf in Havana, but rather anchored in the harbor three-quarters of a mile above the city proper. Passengers and crew alike employed "shore boats" to go ashore or to board a steamer.

Roanoke had reached a point about midway between the anchorage and the city when she was hailed by three small shore boats, each carry a single passenger. The vessel slowed and three men climbed aboard, where they were examined by F. E. Hawley, the steamer's purser.

Brain, using his Johnson alais, was the only member of the trio to have a ticket for the voyage. Upon boarding the steamer he presented a passport which had been visaed by the American Consul in Havana. The others lacked both tickets and passports, but were allowed to purchase tickets on board.

When Brain presented his ticket and passport to Hawley, the latter recognized him as a former Brooklyn schoolmate. Although he hadn't seen Brain in eighteen years, he recognized his facial features on seeing him again.

It is ironic that although a passport and visa system had been instituted shortly after Brain had seized the *Chesapeake* after she left New York Harbor, he somehow obtained a visa and made the security system work for him in Havana.

Brain and his co-conspirators struck at 10 P.M. when the *Roanoke* was approximately 25 miles off the Cuban coast. Dressed in a Confederate naval uniform, Brain stepped on deck and proclaimed in a loud voice, "In the name of the Confederate States of America I demand the surrender of this vessel as a lawful prize!" He then called upon Captain Drew to surrender as a prisoner of war.

Assisted by Master's Mate Thomas R. Little, Purser Alexander Lathrop, and a seaman, Brain captured Captain Drew and the ship's officers on the upper deck and secured them in irons. Henry Parr, along with First Engineer Robert Troth, Second Engineer James Conlen, and three seamen, captured and shackled the rest of the crew on the main deck.

Brain placed purser Lathrop and a seaman in charge of the deck. Joined by mate Little he went below to assist Parr in securing the rest of the ship. Fifty-five minutes after Brain had demanded the the *Roanoke's* surrender, the vessel was his and was proceeding on her voyage as the Confederate state's prize steamship *Roanoke*.

One member of the *Roanoke's* crew, the ship's carpenter, was killed in the attack. He had been captured during the original skirmish, but then made his way back to his cabin, where he obtained an axe from his toolkit.

Slipping out on the main deck, the carpenter swung his axe at Parr and then was shot in the head by one of the hijackers. He dropped the axe and staggered into the engine room, where he was shot at twice. One of the bullets missed, lodging in the arm of the second assistant engineer.

Leaving behind a bloody trail, the mortally wounded carpenter stumbled up to the pilot house and collapsed from loss of blood. He was shot again and killed, and his body hastily thrown overboard.

All of the crew were secured except the firemen and sailors, who were put to work running the vessel. Except for Captain Drew and Purser Hawley, the steamer's officers were paroled, their irons removed during the day and replaced every night.

Brain had the Confederate flag run up the mast, whereupon he posted a notice giving the names and home towns of the *Roanoke's* captors.

> John C. Brain, acting master, Holly Springs, Missouri; H. A. Parr, master's mate, Nashville, Tennessee; Thomas R. Little, master's mate, Mobile, Alabama; Alexander Lathrop, purser, Kentucky; Robert Troth, first engineer, New Orleans; James Conlen, second engineer, Galveston, Texas; Robert Gage, seaman, Mobile, Alabama, Arthur Morehead, seaman, Louisiana; H. J. Braddock, seaman, Union Town, Kentucky and J. D. Van Amburg, Staunton, Virginia.

Brain told the steamer's cabin and steerage passengers that he was taking the *Roanoke* to Bermuda, the closest neutral port, where he planned to land all the officers, crew and passengers. He would then provision and coal his prize and run her past the blockade into Wilmington.

Brain took the time to write a letter, on the *Roanoke's* stationery, to his uncle in England. He described the vessel's capture and commented, "The ship and cargo will be worth £100,000 in the Confederacy. I will post this letter in Bermuda where I call for coals and a pilot and sail for Wilmington, N.C." He told his uncle he would save him a "trophy" of the capture for his office.

The *Roanoke* arrived at St. George, Bermuda on October 4th, where Brain obtained a pilot, who assisted in anchoring the ship offshore at Five Fathom Hole. That afternoon he went ashore on the pilot boat, but returned before dawn the following morning and took the steamer to sea, where it hove to out of sight of land during daylight and returned to a position nearer shore at night.

On October sixth, the *Roanoke* came alongside the *Village Girl*, a local brig, from which she received provisions and about twenty or thirty men, who Brain had hired in St. George to serve aboard the Confederate prize.

The next day the *Roanoke* hove to among the Bermudian island group. Using the steamer's small boats, Brain attempted to transfer provisions and coal from the *Village Girl*. The sea had roughened and his men could only transfer ten or fifteen tons of coal,

About dusk the *Roanoke* steered toward land and made for a brig then working her way out of St. George channel. However, the brig failed to display the pre-arranged signal, a black ball in the topsail and a light in the topmast, and Brain turned his steamer toward another brig, which almost immediately displayed the sought after signal.

The second vessel was the Danish brigantine *Mathilde*, bound for Halifax. Through Confederate agents in St. George, Brain had arranged for the *Mathilde* to meet him offshore so he could transfer the *Roanoke's* officers, crew, and passengers to the neutral vessel.

The transfer of personnel was made, along with $20,000 specie captured aboard the *Roanoke*, and the *Mathilde* set sail for St. George, but due to a lack of wind, anchored at Five Fathom Hole long enough to re-transfer everyone ashore before setting course for Halifax with the money.

Brain, aboard the *Roanake* with his crew and the men he had hired in St. George, had problems. He had recently received information in St. George about the tightening of the Federal blockade along the Southern seaboard. Boldness had always served the former swindler well and he might have been able to run the blockade as John Taylor Wood in the *Tallahassee* had done several weeks previously. However, Brain had been unable to obtain enough coal in Bermuda to make a high-speed run to the coast.

Brain sent his hired men ashore. Thirteen were arrested by the local authorities as soon as they stepped out of their boats.

Brain and the *Roanake's* original captors then set fire to six bales of cotton which had been brought aboard from the brig. When the steamer was well ablaze, they abandoned ship in the remaining small boats. Lacking a pilot, they were nearly lost at sea before being rescued by some fishermen, who brought them ashore at St. George, where they were promptly arrested on charges of piracy.

After three days in the St. George jail, Brain and his group were brought before a magistrate for a probable cause hearing. During the proceeds the magistrate heard five witnesses: Captain Drew and Purser Hawley, who related the events surrounding the *Roanoke's* capture; an inspector of the local police who testified regarding Brain's and his men's arrest; and two men, probably local Confederate shipping or commercial agents, who swore as to the authenticity of the handwriting on Brain's commission and orders. The Crown was represented on the first day of the hearing by S. Brownlow Gray, the Attorney-General, and on the second day and third days by an assistant, Richard Darrell.

Once Brain's commission and orders had been verified, Darrell, withdrew the charge, and Brain and his men were released.

However, Brain and his men were now in trouble with the customs authorities for having brought ashore a quantity of

THE WAR IN VERMONT.

St. Albans Attacked by British Guerrillas.

Three Banks Robbed and Five Citizens Shot.

The Raiders Pursued by Armed Citizens.

BURLINGTON, Vt., Wednesday, Oct. 19.

A party of twenty-five armed men rode into St. Albans this afternoon, and robbed the three banks there of $150,000. It is supposed they were southerners from the border of Canada. Five citizens were shot, one it is thought fatally. Having accomplished their object the band left immediately for Canada.

LATER.—The man, MORRISON, who was shot through the body, has since died.

SECOND DISPATCH.

ST. ALBANS, Vt., Wednesday, Oct. 19.

FROM HAVANA.

The Missing Steamer Roanoke—Her Probable Capture by Rebels.

By the arrival of the *Columbia* we have dates from Havana to Oct. 15.

We learn from a passenger per steamer *Columbia*, arrived to-day from Havana, that an organized plot for the capture of the steamship *Roanoke* existed and was publicly talked of in Havana; and further, that after securing her, the capture of the *Columbia* and the new steamer *Moro Castle* was the programme.

Important Rumors—The Roanoke Captured and Burnt.

HALIFAX, N. S., Wednesday, Oct. 19.

H. M. S. *Steady* reports that it was rumored that the *Roanoke* was captured by the rebel Lieut. BRAINE, who took her to Bermuda and landed the passengers. But he was not allowed coal or provisions. He then proceeded to sea and burnt the *Roanoke* off Bermuda, returning with the crew in boats. He was immediately arrested by the British authorities.

The Pennsylvania Election.

PHILADELPHIA, Wednesday, Oct. 19.

A dispatch from a Harrisburgh correspondent

Two front page stories from *The New York Times*. The left column describes the Confederate raid on St. Albans, Vermont and the right column relates John Clibbon Brain's seizure of the *Roanoke*.

Cuban cigars from the *Roanoke's* cargo. The wily Brain had neglected to pay duty on either the small quantity of cigars he and his men had been smoking around St. George or on the larger quantity stored in a local warehouse. Brain offered to pay the duty retroactively, but the heavy hand of officialdom scorned payment and confiscated the cigars.

A ballad printed as a broadsheet by the *Bermuda Mirror* proclaimed:

> To Captain Brain and Officers we tender our thanks,
> For the cigars they gave us which they bought from the Yanks.
> And although we were willing on them duty to pay,
> John Bull pounced upon them and took them away.
> Now I think it is high time to finish up my song,
> And state though tried for piracy we still did nothing wrong.
> Then three cheers for those Confederates, repeat them far and near,
> I hope they'll burn more Yankee ships, if Abe dont end the war

Once out of the St. George jail, Brain disappeared from Bermuda. Almost two months later he re-appeared in Halifax, where he remained for several days before catching a ship for Nassau, where he dropped out of sight again.

Many of Brain's movements during the Civil War, except during the periods when he was in the public eye and while his daring exploits were being heralded in the press, have been undiscovered and are still shrouded in mystery. Many family documents and letters dealing with his Civil War exploits were destroyed in a May 1940 fire in England.

In his book *The Last of the Privateers*, David Hay of Chesham, England, Brain's cousin, makes a case for Brain's having served with the James River squadron in the desperate defense of Richmond during the Spring of 1865.

Hay thinks Brain was wounded in a skirmish between the James River squadron and the *U.S.S. Omondaga.* Brain himself, in his 1892 *Soldier's Application for Pension* to the State of Tennessee, said he was wounded in the Battle of Bermuda Hundreds on May 26, 1864. In that document, Brain wrote he was wounded "... in the forehead, in the right wrist, the left arm, and through the left side below the heart." Years later, the press frequently commented on Brain's visible scars after covering lectures he was giving throughout the South.

The mystery revolves around when and where Brain was actually wounded. In his pension application he said he was not incapacitated by his wounds and that he was treated by a surgeon in Richmond.

The Bermudas Hundreds action Brain claims to have taken part in took place two days prior to his being granted an appointment as an Acting Master in the Confederate Navy. The wounds Brain received, especially the wound five inches below the heart certainly would have sidelined the naval hijacker for a period of time. There is no doubt that Brain was wounded, the question is on what date were the wounds inflicted and what were the real circumstances?

Press reports later in Brain's life frequently mention his scarred forehead, whereas none of the journalistic accounts of his seizure of the *Roanoke* mention his being scarred, which would have been readily apparent so soon after the action at Bermuda Hundreds.

In a 1903 interview with the *Baltimore Sun* Brain said:

> During the Civil War I was wounded five times ... All the wounds were received in an engagement at the battle of Bermuda Hundred, May 24, 1864. I was at the time in command of a shore battery with 200 seamen under me. In the heat of the engagement I was injured five times in succession as I sat on my horse, but I remained in my saddle until dark. When I dismounted after the battle a negro pulled off my boots and they were almost full of blood.

John Clibbon Brain returned to Richmond in February 1865. According to Brain he was given command of a Confederate naval force bound for San Francisco. The expedition lacked a vessel for the long voyage around Cape Horn, but the resourceful Brain proposed to remedy that problem by cutting out a craft anchored in the East River, which runs into Mobjack Bay on Virginia's eastern shore, adjacent to Chesapeake Bay.

Unable to locate an appropriate vessel, Brain and his men crossed the river to King William County, then to Lancaster

County, where Brain made his headquarters on Dividing Creek, near where it empties into Chesapeake Bay.

With only three days rations among them, the Confederates took possession of a yawl and entered the bay. Off Smith's Point, Virginia they eluded a Union warship which was guarding the Winter Quarter Lightship and then slipped through the coastal blockade by the dark of the moon. They eventually reached Barren Island, off the lower Maryland peninsula, which Brain later said he "...took possession of and held for two days."

A major storm swept the region their second day out. Twenty sailing vessels sought shelter in the Patuxent River across Chesapeake Bay. Brain and his crew waited until midnight, when the storm abated, and early the morning of April 1, 1865, swarmed aboard the 115-ton Baltimore built schooner *St. Mary's*, bound from Baltimore with supplies for the Federal prison at Point Lookout, Maryland.

The schooner was crewed by two white men and twelve blacksand carried six passengers, who were all taken prisoner and placed below decks. The Confederates then abandoned the yawl and made for open sea with their prize.

Off Hog Island, near Cape Charles, Brain and his men captured the *J.B. Spofford*, a schooner from Wicomico, Maryland for New York with a cargo of pine wood. The capture of the *Spofford* was the last capture made by a Confederate vessel along the eastern seaboard.

Brain was unable to handle two vessels, so he bonded the *Spofford* for $25,000, placed the *St. Mary's* original crew and passengers aboard the *Spofford* and released her.

Brain's position was precarious. The last two Confederate ports, Charleston and Wilmington, had been captured by the Union two months previously. Richmond was surrounded. The day after Brain seized the *St. Mary's*, the Confederate Naval Department ordered Rear Admiral Raphael Semmes, commanding the James River Squadron, to destroy his ship and join the forces of General Robert E. Lee. Seven days later, Lee surrendered at Appomatox CoUrt House and for all intents and purposes, the war was over.

Two Confederate vessels remained afloat. One was the *C.S.S. Shenandoah* which was operating against the New

England whaling fleet in the North Pacific. The second was the *St. Mary's*, commanded by John Clibbon Brain, spy, swindler, and hijacker of the *Chesapeake* and the *Roanoke*.

The situation was desperate. He and his crew had no sextant, no charts and no water.

Brain steered his prize southwest-half-west, and eighteen days later sighted the British bark *Stylla*, bound from New York to Matamoras, Mexico, off the Bahamas. He then steered for Nassau, where he was admitted under a plea of distress.

By the time the *St. Mary's* entered Nassau Harbor, Brain and his crew had been reduced to rationing their water, which they had produced by distillation during the voyage, to one pint per man per day.

U.S. Consul Thomas Kirkpatrick in Nassau vigorously protested the action, but the local authorities declined the objection on the grounds the *St. Mary's* was a legitimate prize of war.

The *Bahama Herald* of April 19, 1865, reported:

> Arrival: The Confederate States Prize Schooner *St. Mary's* (Lieut. John C. Brain Commander) arrived at Salt Cays on Monday ... On Captain Brain's producng his commission and orders, His Excellency Gov. Rawson immediately gave orders for her release and kindly granted her permission to remain for the space of twenty-four hours to obtain the necessary supplies of water and wood.

Re-provisioned, Brain sailed the *St. Mary's* out of Nassau and headed for the North-West Providence Channel, the shortest route to the Gulf Stream and the Florida Coast.

Consul Kirkpatrick told the British authorities "(Brain) ... has gone to Spanish Wells or Harbour Islands to get H. A. Paw." It appears that Henry Parr, Brain's able assistant from the *Chesapeake* and *Roanoke* seizures had once again cast his lot with the bold Brain.

On May 9th, Captain Joseph Phillips of the Nassau schooner *Charles Turmell* dropped anchor in Sapadilla Bay, in the Turks and Caicos Islands. Another vessel, which turned out to be the *St. Mary's*, was already in the bay. Phillips had previously been asked by the captain of the *Fawn*, a British gunboat, if he had seen a craft answering the *St. Mary's* description in Bahamian waters.

The next day, Brain himself boarded the *Charles Turmell* and questioned Phillips about any United States or British warships he might have seen or spoken with on his passage from Nassau.

Brain invited Phillips aboard the *St. Mary's* for a drink. While aboard, Phillips noticed a ten-man crew, but the only armament he saw was an old double-barreled fowling gun. However, Phillips afterward reported that the crews of other vessels also anchored in the bay later told him that Brain's crew had been occupying their time cleaning arms and putting cannon balls aboard the schooner.

The *Charles Turmell* sailed on May 9th and the *St. Mary's* slipped out of Sapadilla Bay the following morning and disappeared for a month.

Brain later told the *Baltimore Sun* that he took the *St. Mary's* to Long Island in the Bahamas and secured a gun and a crew of twenty men, then cruised about the islands and captured many small vessels. However, there are apparently no contemporary press or official reports to back up his privateering claim, which was more likely jailhouse boasting on his part.

On June 9th, the *St. Mary's* anchored off Kingston, Jamaica, where Brain and a Lieutenant Edenborough went ashore. The Civil War was over, but the British authorities decided to grant the Confederate Prize Schooner *St. Mary's* normal naval courtesies. They even permitted her to enter the port to obtain supplies.

The *Aboukir*, flagship of the British West Indies squadron, was in port at the time and an officer and boat's crew was sent to inspect the *St. Mary's*. The boarding party reported they found only three old muskets aboard, but a later report stated that armaments and supplies aboard the *St. Mary's* had been sold ashore to purchase passage back to the South for crew members who did not want to go with Brain to England.

Brain's lieutenant told the inspecting party that Brain had not taken his prize into port because the required three months had not passed since the *St. Mary's* had entered a British colonial port. He also said that the crew did not care what happened to their prize, but only wanted to travel to England.

In Kingston, the U.S. Consul was struggling to obtain restitution of Brain's vessel. The British authorites had put the vessel up for sale and the original owners had filed a claim for the craft, further muddying the waters.

Brain apparently abandoned his vessel on June 21st,and boarded a ship for England. The consul in Kingston immediate sent a dispatch to his counterpart in Liverpool,alerting him as to Brain's probable arrival in the United Kingdom.

On July 5, 1865, the Governor of Jamaica solved the problem of the *St. Mary's* by giving the vessel twenty-four hours to leave Jamaican waters.

Other reports indicate that on July 7th, the *St. Mary's* was set on fire between Pedro Cay and the Cayman Islands. Captain Eden of the British armed brigantine *Ruatan* came upon the burning vessel, which had been abandoned by Lieutenant Edenborough and four other Confederates, who were rowing ashore in a small boat. The *Ruatan's* crew, assisted by the Confederates who returned to their vessel, put out the fire and towed the charred hulk to the Cayman Islands, where she was sold for salvage.

CHAPTER SIXTEEN

THE LAST CONFEDERATE PRISONER

John Clibbon Brain visited relatives in England before returning to the United States and settling in Savannah, Georgia, where he attempted to make a living as an artist and illustrator. Although the Civil War was over, Brain's presence in Great Britain had been duly reported to Washington by F. H. Morse, the U.S. Consul in London.

Morse filed a dispatch on December 30, 1865, which stated: "I hear also that J.C. Braine is on his way to the Clyde to take charge of a rebel steamer ... probably a blockade runner."

Brain later returned to Brooklyn, where he had made his home prior to the war. Settling in, he took a room at the Williamsburg House. The local authorities soon learned he was in town, and on September 14, 1866, Benjamin Silliman, the U.S. District Attorney for the Eastern District of New York, contacted the Attorney General in Washington to determine Brain's status.

Silliman cited Brain's seizure of the *Chesapeake* during the recent war and the fact that the steamer's second engineer had been killed and the mate wounded during the vessel's hijacking. Silliman wrote: " I am not aware of any ruling which would require this case to be treated otherwise than as one of murder ... If any decision has been made by the Government which relieves the man from his liability as a criminal may I ask the favor of information to that effect.

EASTERN DISTRICT OF NEW YORK,

U. S. District Attorney's Office,

(18 Court Street,) *Brooklyn, Sept 14th 1866*

Sir,

    I am this day informed of the presence here of a man named <u>Braine</u>, the head of a gang who went on board the Steamer "<u>Chesapeake</u>", as passengers, just as she left on a regular trip for Portland, Dec 5th 1863, and, on the following night, rose upon the officers and crew, killed the second Engineer, wounded the mate, and took possession of the vessel –

    They landed the officers and crew, who found their way to St Johns N. B. They then took the vessel into some bay on the coast of Nova Scotia where she was discovered by the U. S. armed vessel "<u>Ella & Annie</u>" Capt Nichols. When the latter vessel approached, the pirates escaped in the boat. The "<u>Chesapeake</u>" was then taken to Halifax where she was, after proceedings in the Admiralty Court, surrendered to this government, or to her owners

           Braine is stated to be an English=

32

The letter from the U.S. Attorney questioning the Justice Department about John Clibbon Brain's legal status.

Warning that Brain might not be found in case of a delay, the District Attorney requested he be notified by telegraph if Brain should not be arrested.

No reply was received and on the following evening, September 15, 1866, the former swindler, spy and ship-hijacker was arrested at the Wall House in the Williamsburg section of Brooklyn. He was taken to the Forty-fifth Precinct police station, where he was locked up for the night without bedding, although he offered to pay for sheets and a blanket.

In Bermuda John Clibbon Brain had been known as "Bold Brain." Evidence found at the scene of his Brooklyn arrest indicated that the adventuresome former Acting Master in the Confederate Navy had shifted his sights from seizing steamers to seizing an entire island!

Searching Brain's room, the arresting officers discovered a collection of papers and documents which disclosed he had been forming, on paper at least, a filibustering force called the Knights of Arabia. The group's apparent target was the island of Haiti, as indicated by the large number of charts and maps of that location found among his possessions.

The papers included numerous copies of the by-laws of the Knights of Arabia, an embossed parchment oath of allegiance to the Knights, certificates of membership for the group, both blank and filled out; a badge-of-rank as a colonel of the 1st Regiment of the Knights of Arabia and a three-by-five foot, red and blue silk flag with two crescents and a lone white star in the center.

The by-laws required each candidate for membership pay $100 to the Captain of the Company of Knights or to the group's secretary. The secretary in turn would give the candidate a Knights of Arabia bond for $100, with ten percent interest, which was payable ninety days after the filibuster's island target's occupation was recognized by the United States government.

A sheaf of letters between Brain and others included a letter from Henry Parr of Yarmouth, Nova Scotia, which was written on September 9, 1866. In what was obviously a reply to a renewed call to arms from Brain, Parr offered to muster one hundred men for service with the Knights of Arabia if the details and purposes of the Knight's objectives were first explained by the "Commanding General."

The correspondence also included a letter to Brain from the president of the Continental Bank Note Company of New York, who declined to execute an order for the engraving of bonds "unless assured they would in no way be compromised thereby."

Brain was arraigned before U.S. Commissioner Charles W. Newton on September 18, 1866 and charged with "having, along with fourteen accomplices, captured the steamer *Chesapeake* ... and with having killed one of the crew and wounded several others in their efforts... "

W.D. Craft and A. Lathrop, Brain's attorneys, immediately requested additional time to obtain proof that Brain had acted under the orders of superior officers and that he had been a Lieutenant in the Confederate Navy at the time the *Chesapeake* was seized. District Attorney Silliman said he would not object to granting Craft and Lathrop a reasonable amount of time to obtain documents in Brain's defense, but reminded Commissioner Newton the "authority of the so-called Confederate states had never been recognized."

Newton favored a postponement on the grounds that a national question was involved. He did not express an opinion of the cases's merits, but did indicate that the amplest scope of evidence and free discussion should precede any decision regarding the case against Brain.

It was decided to proceed with the examination of prosecution witnesses and then adjourn while the defense sought documents and affidavits on Brain's behalf.

Captain Isaac Willett and three former members of the *Chesapeake's* crew testified as to how Brain and his men had seized the steamer. One of the crew, Samuel H. Seaman, testified Brain had visited the Cromwell line's office at least twice requesting a free pass on the steamer because he was "getting up a directory of the provinces and ... would give a notice of the line if we favored him."

The case was then adjourned and John Clibbon Brain returned to his cell in the King's County Penitentiary, where he remained two years and four months while the Government tried to decide whether to try him for the murder of Orin Schaffer, the *Chesapeake's* second engineer, or whether the act and the *Chesapeake's* seizure had been committed while he held a Confederate commission.

In December 1866, Brain's mother, living outside Montreal with Lucy Hamilton, her married daughter, applied for a pardon for him, which was refused when Secretary of State William Seward recommended it not be granted. Earlier, Seward had said the documents regarding the Knights of Arabia, found at the time of Brain's arrest, did not contain sufficient proof of any "penal act or intention on the part of Brain" to warrant judicial proceedings.

While Brain sat in his cell, his attornies obtained a series of affidavits from former high Confederate naval officers and officials testifying to Brain's status as a Confederate officer acting under official orders.

The former Secretary of the Navy, Stephen R. Mallory, stated: "... I gave to John C. Braine an appointment as a master in the Confederate Navy, together with instructions as to the employment of seamen and as to cruising against the commerce of the United States." However, Mallory failed to help Brain's case any by continuing, "I do not undertake to say positively that he held this appointment in the *Chesapeake* affair, though I am positive that he did when he captured the *Roanoke*, but to the best of my knowledge and belief he held this appointment ... when he captured the *Chesapeake*."

Mallory's statement is vague, as were several other affidavits given in Brain's defense, and ignores the fact that Brain was not actually appointed an Acting Master until almost months after he had seized the *Chesapeake*.

James S. Jones, Registrar of the Confederate Navy Department, gave a deposition in Savannah, Georgia, where he testified to his "own knowledge [Brain] held the position of Acting Master in the Confederate Navy during the year 1863."

Raphael Semmes, commander of the *C.S.S. Alabama* before her destruction by the *U.S.S. Kearsage* off Cherbourg, France, and the commander of the James River Squadron at the time of Richmond's fall, testified he had met Brain at the Navy Department in Richmond and that Brain had worn the uniform of an officer in the Confederate States Navy. Semmes also stated that Brain was generally known throughout the

Raphael Semmes' affidavit regarding John Clibbon Brain's service with the Confederate States Navy.

navy as an officer detailed to capture Union vessels. However, he did not testify Brain was authorized to capture the *Chesapeake*.

John N. Maffitt, commander of the famous Confederate cruiser *C.S.S. Florida* swore he had known Brain during the war and knew him as an officer detailed to "special service." In concluding his deposition regarding his knowledge of Brain, Maffitt said that while he was in command of the steamer *Owl*, in which he ran the blockade from Bermuda several times, he had conveyed Brain to the Confederate lines.

These affidavits failed to free Brain from jail, or to resolve the question as to whether he was acting as an officer in the Confederate Navy when he seized the *Chesapeake*.

Neither Brain or his attorneys reminded Commissioner Newton that the defendant actually had held two appointments, an illegal one granted by Vernon Locke, a British subject, given him so he could seize the *Chesapeake*, and a legal one granted by Secretary of the Navy Stephen Mallory, so he could seize the *Roanoke*.

Brain stayed in the penitentiary for twenty-eight months, untried and unconvicted. Late in his imprisonment he was interviewed by a reporter from the *New York Tribune*, who compared Brain to the fictional Philip Nolan, the "Man Without a Country."

Pipe in hand, Brain spun the reporter a tale of his wartime activities, which highlighted certain actions and obscured others. Brain said his commission had been written on fly-sheet note paper and was either worn out or lost. He claimed to have received orders from the Navy Department to go north in June of 1863 and seize a steamer on the high seas.

Defending his actions, Brain claimed, "I wish to make a clear and unequivocal statement that in every capture I made, private property was scrupulously respected and human life never heedlessly sacrificed."

He said he was in command of the Confederate schooner *St. Mary's* at the end of the war, but neglected to say he had seized her on Chesapeake Bay. He claimed to have returned to the United States in October 1865, " ... trusting to security to [the protection of] President Lincoln's Proclamation of Amnesty."

The reporter closed his article with a vivid impression of
Brain and the effects on his physical being caused by so many
months in a dark and damp cell:

> Lieut. Brain was a tall, straight and commanding personage
> when in health, but his sufferings in prison have been so
> intense that he cannot walk without the aid of a crutch, and is,
> perhaps, permanently disabled. His right foot is much swollen
> from inflammatory rheumatism, a disease he attributes to the
> unavoidable dampness of the prison, and he is indeed a wreck
> of the man who entered it nearly three years ago. He is only 29
> years of age ... A widowed mother and two young daughters
> depend upon him for support and he expresses himself as
> anxious to be with them. Efforts are being made to secure his
> pardon at the hands of President Johnson, but if he is not
> pardoned, the Constitution guarantees him a speedy trial ...

This and other newspaper accounts of Brain's situation
began to bring pressure on the government in Washington to
either bring Brain to trial or free him.

A public campaign began in Baltimore and across the South
to obtain the freedom of John Clibbon Brain, who the press
began to call "The Last Confederate Prisoner of War."

Early in January 1869, Algernan S. Sullivan, Brain's
attorney in New York, wrote the Attorney General in
Washington to report a man claiming to be Brain's brother had
appeared at his office with two depositions regarding Brain's
physical condition. Discussing the depositions, Sullivan told
the Attorney General, "They show a pitiable state for Braine
(sic), and believe me, were it not so, I would not venture again
to tax your patience with another letter on the subject."

John Zabriski, the jail doctor, commented in his statement:

> He [Brain] is at present suffering from an ulcerated foot and
> leg which compel the use of a crutch in walking. He has [a]
> constant sore throat and is subject to constant ulceration in
> various parts of his body. His general health has been lacking
> for some time and the probabilities are that it will continue to do
> so as long as his confinement is prolonged.

The second statement submitted to the Attorney General by
Brain's attorney was written by a New Yorker by the name of

A. M. Foute, who had been visiting Brain during his two year imprisonment. Foute, who had no apparent prior connection with Brain, said he was interested in the prisoner because of "what I deem to be my duty to suffering humanity."

Regarding Brain's health, Foute reported:

> He has lost all appetite and is rapidly wasting away, indeed is now a most pitiable object, and one worthy of clemency and mercy. He has now suffered more than two years imprisonment for his offense, part of that time in a close cell.
>
> I would therefore most respectfully ask that his case may receive prompt attention at your hands, and if possible that an order for his discharge may be issued ... if not release from prison, death, will soon give him the discharge, we know beg in behalf of a suffering fellow creature.

During January and February 1869 the campaign to obtain Brain's release brought pressure directly on President Andrew Johnson in the White House. A group of fifty New Orleans women petitioned the President for his release, claiming "... he committed no act of murder, himself, but held for the act of another, out of his presence, and which was strictly an act of war."

The New Orleans action preceded one from a large group of Baltimore women who pointed out Brain's failing health and said "his hair is silvered with grey at the early age of twenty-nine."

They told the President:

> His family needs his counsel and care while they pine, for the opportunity to afford him, the tender offices of affection which his condition demands. The women of Baltimore ... have ministered to his bodily wants as far as they could and have aided in clothing and feeding his sorrowing household in their stricken Southern home. Is it not enough that he and they have suffered so long and so severely?

As President Johnson prepared for an official visit to Baltimore, the ladies made one final, impassioned plea:

> Let him go free to his home and friends, so that when you visit at Baltimore, there will remain not one solitary sufferer behind you - that the glad sounds of welcome with which you

will be greeted by us shall not be rendered discordant by the
wail of anguish which will fall upon your ears from the distant
cell of the solitary captive.

On February 26, 1869 the U.S. Attorney General States
ruled "noelle prosequi" in the case of John Clibbon Brain, and
the man the New York *Herald Tribune* had called "The Man
Without A Country" hobbled through the massive doors of
the King's County Penitentiary and headed north to Canada.

At Longueuil, near Montreal, Brain visited his mother and
Lucy Hamilton. Later he returned to Savannah, Georgia,
where he again attempted to support himself and his family as
an illustrator.

Little is certain of his activities in Georgia during the next
decade or more. About 1886, he was purported to be
promoting "industrial properties," which probably meant the
former swindler had hit upon hard times and had reverted to
his pre-war scams.

In 1891, Brain and his wife moved to Knoxville, Tennessee,
where he obtained "scant support" operating a small
restaurant called The Owl. However, this enterprise failed to
provide him sufficient support and a year later the aging
veteran applied for, and received, a pension from the State of
Tennessee based on his Confederate service.

Brain had been wounded at the Battle of Bermuda
Hundreds, Virginia, which he mentioned in his pension
application, but he based the bulk of his claim on the physical
debilitation caused by the postwar imprisonment in his damp
Brooklyn cell. In reply to a question about alcohol usage, he
wrote, "I take a drink occasionally, but was never drunk in my
life."

The pension was granted, but was revoked several years
later when the roll of pensioners was trimmed to meet a
smaller legislative appropriation. Dr. S.P. Hood, who had
examined the aging *Chesapeake* hijacker for the original
pension application, examined Brain and reported:

> Almost helpless. Condition worse than when pension was
> granted. The wound in left-side below the heart is now causing
> more trouble. The feet drawn and deformed by reason [of] close
> confinement are worse so that walking is more difficult. The
> physical condition is weaker.

Brain told the examiners his only property consisted of one set of bedroom furniture, a carpet, an old range, and a few commodity jars, of all which, he swore, would sell for about $25 at auction. He said he had been forced to close The Owl "owing to the hard times."

Brain lost his pension and then did what he had done so many times before ... he hit the road. For several years he traveled the South, lecturing on his wartime exploits. His posters proclaimed "All proceeds of these Lectures are forwarded to the Jefferson Davis Monument Association at Richmond, Va." Such an association did exist in Richmond, and was raising funds for a monument to the revered Confederate president, but no one in it had ever heard of John Clibbon Brain, nor had anyone there ever received funds from him. Soon, Confederate veteran's publications were circulating reports warning of the silver-haired Brain's new dodge.

In Austin, Texas, Brain advertised for ladies to travel with him and sing at his lectures. One Texas journal reported, "This battle-scarred veteran (?) excited the sympathy of Confederates and was treated with due courtesy wherever he went."

In January 1903, Brain was arrested in Baltimore for non-payment of a $41.22 hotel bill at the Eutaw House. Locked up at the Western Police Station, he told arresting officers he was a chemist and president of the Standard Fertilizer Company of Birmingham, Alabama, and that he had been a commander in the Confederate Navy during the Civil War.

The press discovered the aging veteran's plight and Brain briefly basked in the limelight, recounting tales of when he had captured the *Chesapeake* and the *Roanoke*. One reporter researched Brain's story in Scharf's *History of the Confederate States Navy*, only to have Brain say "The history in the main is correct, but there are many features that Scharf did not know ...". Brain claimed to have received a commission and orders from Secretary Mallory to seize the *Chesapeake* and said the capture of the *Roanoke* was the more difficult of his two major captures.

Ragsdale's Opera House.

JACKSONVILLE, TEXAS,

Saturday Evening, Jan. 18th,

AT 7:30 O'CLOCK.

BENEFIT OF THE

Jefferson = Davis

MONUMENT.

COMMANDER

John C. Brain,

Formerly of the C. S. Navy,

The Last Prisoner of the War,

Will Deliver his Famous and Interesting

LECTURE

ON THE FOLLOWING SUBJECTS:

The Capture of S. S. "Chesapeake," out of New York Harbor, Dec. 5, 1863.

Capture of U. S. M. S. S. "Roanoke," off the Island of Cuba, Sept. 29, 1864.

Last Confederate Naval Expedition, which left Richmond, Va., Feb. 27, 1865, under orders for San Francisco, Cal.

The Capture of St. Mary's off Pautexen River Chesapeake Bay, April 1, 1865; cruise of the vessel and her destruction off the Island of Jamaica, June 19, 1865. With many amusing incidents.

Collection will be taken up for the benefit of the Jefferson Davis Monument Fund.

All the proceeds of these Lectures are forwarded to the Jefferson Davis Monument Association, at Richmond, Va.

Banner Steam Print, Jacksonville, Texas.

David Hay

A poster advertising John Clibbon Brain's lecture in Jacksonville, Texas.

Brain's shining armor became somewhat tarnished when one detective Thomas reported he had investigated the old Confederate's background and found the Standard Fertilizer Company had no commercial rating in Birmingham and didn't even have a plant in that city. He also reported that Brain held most of the firm's stock and that the remaining small amount was held by persons of "no business standing", to which Brain had given the stock.

Brain rebutted Thomas' claims by protesting his company had only been formed the previous April. He said it was true his firm had no plant in Birmingham, but claimed it did have one in Bessemer, which had not yet begun operations.

Thomas recounted how Brain had previously given shares of his stock to a hotel keeper in payment of his bill. He then offered evidence which indicated that twelve years previously Brain had stayed at Baltimore's Carrolton House, where he had also presented stock as payment for his room.

Confronted with two entries under his name in a book published to warn hotel keepers against fraudulent guests, Brain said he did not remember stopping at one of the establishments mentioned, and protested he had been forced to leave the second when the owner closed it. He admitted he did not have the money to pay his bill at the time the hotel closed, but claimed he would have met his obligation if he had been given the opportunity.

The police wanted Brain photographed for the rogue's gallery, but the presiding judge prohibited the action and said, "I do not propose to have the man branded guilty and his photograph scattered about the country until it has been proved beyond the question that he merits it." The case likely collapsed shortly thereafter, because it soon disappeared from the newspapers.

Although he was a charming swindler for most of his life, it should be remembered that during the Civil War, John Clibbon Brain successfully seized at least four vessels in the name of the Confederate States Navy, although the *Chesapeake* seizure was piracy without legal authority. He also successfully and tied up numbers of Union warships along the eastern seaboard as they scoured the waters in search of him. He paid for his boldness by ruining his health in a dark and damp jail cell.

John Clibbon Brain died a pauper in Tampa, Florida, in 1906.

CHAPTER SEVENTEEN

AFTER THE SILENCE

While John Clibbon Brain's life following the Civil War was one of imprisonment, unfullfilled dreams and poverty, the other Confederates who operated in and around Maine generally fared differently. Most resumed the patterns of their pre-war lives, although not always in their pre-war locations.

* * *

William Collins signed an oath of allegiance to the United States on July 19, 1865. Then he returned to the Morrow Plantation at Richlands, Mississippi and began the slow process of helping rebuild the plantation which had slid into decline during the war.

Not long afterwards Collins heard a rumor there was money to be made in the Florida orange groves and he left Mississippi to try his hand in the citrus growing business.

While in Florida he rekindled an old interest in sailing and sport fishing. He had learned the rudiments of handling a small boat as a boy in Nova Scotia. One day he rented a small sail boat and set out alone. In the late afternoon he found himself several miles off shore facing of a stiffening southwest wind. He tried to beat his way back to shore, but the wind, actually the fringes of an approaching hurricane, relentlessly pushed push his tiny boat out into the Gulf Stream.

The storm lasted three days and nights and carried Collins many miles from his point of departure. What little food and water he had taken with him was soon gone. When the gale finally abated he was able to raise a crude distress signal. Several vessels passed near his small craft without seeing it. Eventually, a full-rigged Spanish ship spotted him.

None of the Spanish sailors, who were returning to their homeland with a cargo of molasses, spoke a word of English. Collins, had studied Spanish in New York before the war and was able to explain how he had been blown to sea while fishing. He apologized that he had no money, but said he would gladly work his passage to Europe as a seaman.

Arriving in Spain, the former Calais Bank raider began a grand continental tour. He traveled about Spain, then visited Italy and Greece, and continued as far southeast as Egypt and Palestine. He returned to the United States by way of England, where he visited London, Oxford and Cambridge. He cleared customs at Boston and headed for Fryeburg, Maine to visit his brother, the Reverend William Collins. When he eventually arrived back at Richlands, he discovered his Mississippi friends had presumed he was dead.

William Collins was a visionary most of his life. Mallie Morrow, who was born at Richlands in 1860, wrote about her memories of "Captain Collins" in 1938. At that time she remarked, "He was a cordial and loving companion, deeply interested in literature in all its branches and familiar with the Koran as with the Bible, although the latter was studied for critcism alone. ... Being visionary [he] never succeeded in his small investments, but accumulated sufficiently from his place in the store to do the things he most wanted to do and that was to travel ... "

The former Confederate naval officer settled down at Richlands to work in the plantation store and to maintain a flock of one hundred sheep. Later, he added a like number of goats to his holdings.

An epidemic of yellow fever spread into Mississippi from Louisiana, necessitating a quarantine in the former state, which prevented all travel across the state line. Collins, however, was undeterred by the quarantine. He decided to escape the epidemic by walking to Chicago where another

William Collins, sometime after the Civil War.

brother, Robert, owned a harness-making business. William Collins walked out of Mississippi, across Tennessee, Kentucky, and Illinois to Chicago, where Robert gave him a job in his firm until it was safe to return to Richlands.

Few of Collins' investments produced a solid return. Late in his life he bought a tract of land near Richlands at a tax sale. But the land was mostly swamp and never yielded the timber crop he had envisioned when he purchased it. The swampy land was full of malaria and Collins finally came down with chills and a fever which finally killed him. He died in 1887. The sale of his land netted only enough to pay for his headstone in the Morrow family cemetery when his estate was settled.

* * *

The Reverend John Collins spent the years following the Civil War serving a variety of small Methodist churches throughout Maine. He wrote at least one newspaper article about the part he played in foiling the Confederate raid on the Calais bank. Later, he presented a regimental flag once owned by his brother William to the Maine Historical Society in Portland.

In 1909 he endeavored to promote an old hymn, "In God We Trust", first published in 1869, as a new national hymn. Latham True, a Portland composer, wrote a tune to go with the old hymn and Reverend Collins copyrighted the work in 1910 and sold it from his Portland home for ten cents a sheet.

He preached for the last time at Portland's Chestnut Street Methodist Church on January 20, 1914. He died September 8th, that year, at the age of eighty-two and was buried in Somersworth, New Hampshire. His last words were, "I want to vote at the election for prohibition ..."

* * *

After his release from the Maine State Prison in Thomaston, Francis X. Jones returned to St. Louis. In 1866 he was the local city directory as a "clerk."

In 1901, he applied for admission to the the Confederate Home of Missouri in Higginsville. Superintendent George E.

Janae Fuller
Francis X. Jones' gravestone at the Confederate Memorial Site, Higginsville, Missouri.

Patton, querying the Record and Pension office in Washington regarding Jones' military background, wrote: "The old man is somewhat demented, and incoherent, but bears very complimentary recommendations, as to his honor and integrity ..."

The reply from the pension office stated Francis Xavier Jones had been a corporal in Company D, Bowen's First Missouri Infantry, Confederate Army. The information from Washington failed to disclose both Jones' activities as a Confederate dispatch carrier and as one of the Calais Bank raiders.

The Confederate Home of Missouri was demolished in 1950 and its location is now a Confederate Memorial Historic site. The Calais Bank raider's headstone stands proudly among those of other Confederates buried in the old cemetery there.

* * *

John Quay Howard returned to his native Ohio following his return to the United States from his wartime post in St.John, New Brunswick. From 1867 until 1871 he was a part owner and editor of the *Ohio State Journal*. In 1876, he married Florence A. Leach of Springfield, Ohio, and became an editorial writer for the *New York Tribune*. He wrote a series of articles championing Rutherford B. Hayes' bid for the White House. As he previously had done for Abraham Lincoln, Howard wrote a campaign biography of Hayes. Later he authored a history of the Louisiana Purchase.

In 1880, he was appointed chief customs appraiser for the New York area. Afterwards he served two years as a special agent of the United States Census.

He joined the staff of the Library of Congress in 1894, where his original assignment was in the copyright division. In 1897, he was placed in charge of the Congressional Reference Library, a post he held until his death in 1912.

J.Q. Howard suffered a fatal stroke at six o'clock in the morning, November 15, 1912 at his family home in The Brunswick Apartments. He was seventy-six years old. His funeral was held at the family apartment and interment followed at Rock Creek Cemetery

* * *

Paroled from his Fort Warren cell, Charles W. Read served with the James River Squadron in the defense of Richmond. In March 1865, he took command of the ram C.S.S. *William H. Webb* on Louisiana's Red River. The war was drawing to a close, but the bold Read readied his craft and prepared to take her out of the Red River and dash 300 miles down the Mississippi River, past New Orleans, to the open Gulf.

On April 23rd, Read, under forced draft, astounded three Union blockade vessels by steaming into the Mississippi. A running battle followed as Read out-distanced his pursuers, who had originally mistaken the white-hulled *Webb* for a Union vessel.

Outrunning additional pursuers, Read paused only long enough to cut riverside telegraph lines in a unavailing effort to delay Union forces responding to reports of his audacious dash to sea. Just above New Orleans, Read had his vessel's steam pressure brought up to maximum, then ordered a United States flag raised to half-staff in mourning for President Lincoln's death.

Plunging ahead at full speed, the *Webb* passed New Orleans at midnight, April 24, 1865. A group of Union gunboats opened fire on the *Webb* whereupon Read terminated his use of the U. S. flag and ordered a Confederate banner hoisted aloft. The Union vessels' fire hit Read's craft three times, but failed to blunt the Confederate ship's thrust.

Twenty-five miles below New Orleans, Read's brazen charge halted when the *Webb* got caught in a squeeze between her pursuers and the U.S.S. *Richmond*, which was beating up river to cut off the Confederate vessel.

Read ordered the *Webb* run aground and set afire, then he and his men scurried ashore and plunged into the nearby swamps in a final escape attempt. Their effort proved futile, as they were soon rounded up and taken to New Orleans, where they were demeaned by a public display before being paroled and freed to return to their homes.

The bodacious Charles W. Read became a pilot at Southwest Pass, one of the mouths of the Mississippi River, a profession he followed until his death.

* * *

John Taylor Wood fled Richmond with President Jefferson Davis and his cabinet, who intended to establish a new seat of the Confederacy in Danville, Virginia. Pursuring Union forces drove the Davis party further and further South. Union cavalry surrounded and captured President Davis and his party at Irwinville, Georgia on May 10, 1865.

Afraid his reputation as a raider would cause him to be singled out for special treatment, Wood determined to escape. Biding his time, he bribed a guard with two twenty-dollar gold pieces. The soldier simply turned his back as Wood quietly walked into the underbrush surrounding the camp and disappeared into a nearby swamp.

Cautiously, Wood worked his way south, eventually crossing into Florida, where he encountered a small group of

John Taylor Wood.

fleeing Confederates. Procuring a small boat, the men attempted to sail east way to the Bahamas. However, the coastal currents proved to be too strong and the small party instead turned south toward Cuba, where they arrived June 11, 1865.

United in their escape, the former Confederates quickly went their separate ways, each setting off to make a new life for himself. Wood decided to establish a new home in Halifax, Nova Scotia, where he arrived on June 30, 1865. Pausing a few days in the Nova Scotian city to savor his new freedom, Wood withdrew $100 from the *Tallahasseee's* old account and then traveled on to Montreal, where he was joined by his wife and two of their children.

In Montreal Wood and his wife decided to return to Halifax and make their home in that maritime city, where Wood immediately established himself as a leading citizen in the community. Wood went into partnership with Captain John Wilkinson, a famous blockade runner, and the pair founded Wilkinson, Wood & Company, a merchant commision house. When Wilkinson returned to the South, Wood continued the firm as Wood & Company. He soon became active in the Eastern Steamship Company, which was formed to develop trade between Halifax and Newfoundland. Later, the former Confederate became secretary of the Halifax Pilot Commission.

Two of Wood's sons, Charles and Zachary, continued the family's military tradition. After graduating from the Royal Military College at Kingston, Ontario, each forged a distinguished career. Charles served in India and later in South Africa during the Boer War, and was the first Canadian killed in that conflict. Zachary fought in the campaigns against the Indians during the Northwest Rebellion, then distinguished himself in service with the Royal Canadian Mounted Police.

Over the years, Wood occasionally returned to the United States, usually to attend Confederate memorial functions. However, he always returned home to Halifax, where he was an honored and respected member of the community. He died of rheumatism July 19, 1904.

Possibly because of his pre-war backgound and education, John Taylor Wood became the best established of the Confederates who had plagued Maine during the war. He stayed loyal to the idea and ideals of the Confederacy long after the guns were silent and others had returned to their homes. On occasion, John Taylor Wood proudly flew the stars and bars flag from the staff atop Wood & Company.

BIBLIOGRAPHY

PRIMARY MATERIALS

Records

The chapters dealing with the seizure of the *Caleb Cushing*, the capture of the *Chesapeake* and the cruise of the *C.S.S. Tallahassee* were written after consulting the most useful and accessible source *The Offical Records of the Union and Confederate Navies in the War of the Rebellion* (31 vols.; Washington, 1894-1927).

In addition, *The War of the Rebellion: A Compilation of the Official Records of the Union and Confederate Armies* (128 vols.; Washington, 1880-1901) the companion set, was consulted regarding the Confederate attack on St. Albans, Vermont

The Department of State's *Papers Relating To Foreign Affairs* (2 vols.; Washington, 1866) was consulted regarding the seizure of the *Chesapeake* and United States - British relations.

Manuscripts

This book draws heavily on two small manuscript collections. The *Turner-Baker Papers* in the National Archives includes most of the documents held by the U.S. Government dealing with the Calais Bank raid. This small file includes Francis X. Jones' letters to his mother and his landlady; his notes to the Washington County Sheriff and the county attorney; letters from the sheriff to Judge Advocate General Joseph Holt and Secretary of War Edwin Stanton; Levi C. Turner's reports to Holt and Stanton and a copy of a letter from William Collins to his sister.

Other National Archives collections contain documents dealing with the Calais Bank raid. Francis X. Jones's letter to President Abraham Lincoln can be found in Record Group 107. Dispatches sent to the Secretary of State by J. Q. Howard, US Consul General at St. John, New Brunswick, are contained in Record Group 59. These include Dispatch No.72, which informed the Secretary a rebel force was being formed to raid the frontier and Dispatch No. 73 which notified the Secretary the raiders had been arrested at Calais and included a newspaper clipping about the raid.

William Daymond's file in the Military Service Branch, Military Archives Division of the National Archives includes several Confederate documents dealing with his capture and imprisonment after he deserted from his New Jersey regiment. The file also includes a copy of the military orders granting him a pardon for the part he played in the Calais Bank raid.

The second manuscript collection dealing directly with the raid is the group of materials I have termed *The Collins Papers* . This small, but important collection, includes papers and documents collected by the Reverend John Collins and other members of the Collins family. The collection is currently in the possession of Dorothea Collins of Chebeague Island, Maine and New Jersey.

This unique collection includes several letters written by William Collins from both the Washington County Jail at Machias and the Maine State Prison at Thomaston; a letter recommending William Collins be appointed to the Confederate Navy; the actual document appointing Collins an Acting Master in the Confederate Navy; William Collins's pass through the lines issued by Stephen R. Mallory, Secretary of the Confederate Navy; and a letter written by Mallory saying he would tell the Confederate exchange officer to notify his Federal counterpart that William Collins was a Confederate naval officer.

The collection also includes two carte de visite photographs of William Collins in the uniform of an officer of the Confederate Army.

In addition, the collection includes the typescript of an article written by Reverend John Collins and letters written to Reverend Collins by former officers of the Maine State Prison. It also includes a typescript about William Collins by Ensign Bertrand R. T. Collins, USN, the father of Dorothea Collins. This typescript deals with William Collins, his service with the Confederate Army and his part in the raid on Calais, Maine.

The collection also includes two letters written to Ensign Collins in 1938 by Mrs. R. E. Wilburn of Lexington, Kentucky. Mrs. Wilburn was the former Mallie Morrow, of Richlands, Mississippi. William Collins had worked for her father and she wrote about her childhood memories of the former Confederate raider. Her second letter includes material about Collins' activities and travels in the years after the Civil War.

Materials dealing with John Clibbon Brain's 1866 arrest and imprisonment in the Brooklyn (NY) Penitentiary are located at the National Archives in Record Group 60, Records of the Department of Justice. The collection includes the affidavits submitted in Brain's defense by former Confederate officials.

The chapters dealing with Charles R. Read and the cruise of the *Florida No. 2* and the destruction of the *Caleb Cushing* are based primarily on the previously cited *Official Records of the Union and Confederate Navies* and contemporary newspaper accounts. The log of the *Tacony*, maintained by her Confederate captors, is located in the National Archives, Record Group 45.

SECONDARY MATERIALS

Books

Baker, L. C., *History of the United States Secret Service*.Published by L. C. Baker, King & Baird, Printers, Philadelphia, 1867.

Beale, Howard K., Editor, *Diary of Gideon Welles*, 3 Vols., W. W. Norton & Co., New York, 1960.

Benjamin, L. N., *The St. Albans Raid, Investigation Into The Charges, etc.*, John Lovell, printer, Montreal, 1865.

Boykin, Edward, *Ghost Ship of The Confederacy*, Funk & Wagnalls, New York, 1957.

_____, *Sea Devil of The Confederacy*, Funk & Wagnalls, New York, 1959.

Davis, Burke, *Our Incredible Civil War*, Holt, Rinehart & Winston, New York, 1960.

Hay, David & Joan, *The Last of the Confederate Privateers*, Crown Publishers, New York, 1977.

Headley, John, *Confederate Operations in Canada & New York*, Neale Publishing Co., New York, 1906.

Horan, James D., *Confederate Agent, A Discovery in History*, Crown Publishers, New York, 1954.

Horner, Dave, *The Blockade-Runners*, Dodd, Mead & Co., New York, 1968.

Kinchen, Oscar A., *Daredevils of The Confederate Army*, Christopher Publishing, Boston, 1959.

Klement, Frank L., *Dark Lanterns*, Louisiana State University, Baton Rouge, 1984.

Moore, Frank, *The Rebellion Record*, D. Van Nostrand, New York, 1865.

Robinson, Jr., William Morrison, *The Confederate Privateers*, Yale University Press, New Haven, 1928.

Ritchie, Mr. Justice, *The Chesapeake, The Case of David Collins, et al.*, J. &. A. McMillan, printers, St. John, N. B., 1864.

Singleton, Royce Gordan, *John Taylor Wood*, University of Georgia, Athens, Ga., 1979.

Snow Edward Rowe, *The Romance of Casco Bay*, Dodd, Mead & Co., New York, 1975.

____, *The Romance of Boston Bay*, Yankee Publishing Co., Boston, 1944.

____, *The Islands of Boston Harbor*, Dodd, Mead & Co., New York, 1971.

Stern, Philip Van Doren, *Secret Missions of the Civil War*, Bonanza Books, New York, 1959.

____, *The Confederate Navy*, Bonanza Books, New York, 1962.

Wells, Tom Henderson, *The Confederate Navy, A Study in Organization*, University of Alabama, University, Al., 1971

Winks, Robin, *Canada and the United States, The Civil War Years*, John Hopkins Press, Baltimore, 1960.

Articles

"Betrayed Brother For His Country," *Lewiston Journal Magazine*, May, 1910.

"Who Is Commander J. C. Brain," *Confederate Veteran*, October, 1896.

Alexander, Capt. J. W., "How We Escaped From Fort Warren," *New England Magazine*, October, 1892.

Andrews, Roland Franklyn, "How 'Unpreparedness' Undid St. Albans," *The Outlook*, November, 1916.

Bovey, Wilfred, "Confederate Agents in Canada During the American Civil War, " *Canadian Historical Review, March*, 1921.

Holbrook, Stewart, "The St. Albans Raid, " *American Mercury*, June, 1946.

Smith, Mason Philip, "Confederate Raid on Calais," *DownEast Magazine*, August, 1966.

Wood, John Taylor, "The 'Tallahassee's' Dash Into New York Waters," *Century Magazine*, July, 1898.

Newspapers

Augusta (Maine) *Kennebec Journal*
Bangor (Maine) *Whig & Courier*
Boston (Massachusetts) *Daily Advertiser*
Brunswick (Maine) *Telegraph*
Eastport (Maine) *Sentinel*
Ellsworth (Maine) *American*
Halifax (Nova Scotia) *Nova Scotian*

Lewiston (Maine) *Journal*
Louisville (Kentucky) *Courier-Journal*
Machais (Maine) *Union*
Montreal (Quebec) *Montreal Herald*
———— Commercial Advertiser
New York Herald
New York Times
New York Daily Tribune
Portland (Maine) *Portland Advertiser*
———— *Eastern Argus*
———— *Evening Express*
———— *Maine Sunday Telegram*
———— *Press Herald*
———— *Transcript*
Presque Isle (Maine) *The Loyal Sunrise*
St. John (New Brunswick) *Daily Evening Globe*
———— *Daily Morning Telegraph*
———— *The Morning Freeman*
———— *The Morning News*

Index

CONFEDERATES DOWNEAST was set in 11 point Palatino by Intergraphics, Inc., Alexandria, Virginia. It was printed on 60 lb. Glatfelter, natural, acid-free paper by Thomson-Shore, Inc., Dexter, Michigan. The cover was designed by Richard Vieira, New Gloucester, Maine, who also selected the text type. The book was designed and published by The Provincial Press, Portland, Maine.